Table of Contents

Introduction 6
The Diversity of Conflict Scenarios 6
Adapting Conflict Resolution Strategies to Context 10
Leveraging Your Skillset for Varied Situations 14

Chapter 1: Navigating Workplace Conflicts 18
Understanding Conflict Dynamics in the Workplace 18
Addressing Conflicts with Colleagues 22
Resolving Conflicts with Supervisors and Managers" the sub topic for about 3000 words long 26
Strategies for Harmonious Team Collaboration 31

Chapter 2: Family Dynamics and Relationships 35
Unraveling Family Conflicts: Roots and Patterns 35
Addressing Parent-Child Conflicts Constructively 39
Sibling Rivalry and Conflict Resolution Strategies 43
Nurturing Healthy Relationships Within Extended Family 47

Chapter 3: Intimate Relationships and Partnerships 51
Conflict's Role in Intimate Relationships 51
Addressing Trust Issues and Jealousy 56
Conflict Resolution in Differing Value Systems 61
Strategies for Maintaining Intimacy Through Conflict 65

Chapter 4: Navigating Friendships and Social Circles 69
Handling Conflicts Among Friends 69
Managing Group Dynamics and Conflicts in Social Circles 73
Balancing Personal Boundaries and Social Connections ... 76
Strengthening Bonds Through Constructive Conflict Resolution 79

Chapter 5: Promoting Understanding in Communities 82
Conflict in Diverse Community Settings 82
Engaging in Constructive Dialogues with Varied Groups . 85
Addressing Socio-Political Conflicts with Empathy 88
Fostering Harmony in Local and Global Communities 91

Chapter 6: Applying Conflict Resolution to Online Interactions 94
Navigating Conflicts in the Digital Age 94
Resolving Misunderstandings in Virtual Communication. 97
Addressing Online Bullying and Harassment 100
Promoting Positive Interactions in Online Communities. 103

Chapter 7: Conflict as Catalyst for Societal Change 106
Harnessing Conflict for Positive Transformation 106

Copyright © 2023 by Jonathan T. Morgan (Author)

All rights reserved. No part of this book may be reproduced or utilized in any form or by any means, electronic or mechanical, including photocopying, recording or by any information storage and retrieval system, without permission in writing from the publisher, except for brief quotations in critical articles or reviews.

The content of this book is based on various sources and is intended for educational and entertainment purposes only. While the author has made every effort to ensure the accuracy, completeness, and reliability of the information provided, the information may be subject to errors, omissions, or inaccuracies. Therefore, the author makes no warranties, express or implied, regarding the content of this book.

Readers are advised to seek the guidance of a licensed professional before attempting any techniques or actions outlined in this book. The author is not responsible for any losses, damages, or injuries that may arise from the use of information contained within. The information provided in this book is not intended to be a substitute for professional advice, and readers should not rely solely on the information presented.

By reading this book, readers acknowledge that the author is not providing legal, financial, medical, or professional advice. Any reliance on the information contained in this book is solely at the reader's own risk.

Thank you for selecting this book as a valuable source of knowledge and inspiration. Our aim is to provide you with insights and information that will enrich your understanding and enhance your personal growth. We appreciate your decision to embark on this journey of discovery with us, and we hope that this book will exceed your expectations and leave a lasting impact on your life.

Title: Conflict Resolution in Various Settings
Subtitle: Family Bonds and Disagreements: A Path to Healing

Series: Harmony Within: Mastering Conflict Resolution
Author: Jonathan T. Morgan

Advocating for Social Justice through Conflict Resolution *109*
Collaborative Efforts for Change in Larger Societal Conflicts *112*
Using Lessons from Conflict to Shape a More Equitable Future *115*
Conclusion **118**
Reflecting on the Diversity of Conflict Resolution Challenges *118*
Equipped to Address Conflict in All Areas of Life *121*
The Ongoing Journey to Becoming a Master Conflict Resolver *124*
Wordbook **128**
Supplementary Materials **132**

Introduction
The Diversity of Conflict Scenarios

Conflict is an inevitable part of human interaction, arising from the diversity of perspectives, needs, and desires that characterize our lives. From the mundane disagreements to the complex societal clashes, conflicts manifest in various forms, and they permeate every facet of our existence. Understanding the diverse landscape of conflict scenarios is crucial for navigating these challenges effectively and promoting harmonious resolutions.

In this introductory chapter, we delve into the multifaceted nature of conflicts, exploring the wide range of settings where they arise and the unique dynamics that underpin each scenario. By recognizing the complexity and nuances of these conflicts, we set the stage for the exploration of adaptable conflict resolution strategies that can be applied across different contexts.

Conflict Across Life's Spectrum: An Overview

To comprehend the diversity of conflict scenarios, one must first acknowledge that conflicts extend across a spectrum, ranging from personal relationships to community dynamics to global issues. What sets the stage for these conflicts are the individual and collective perspectives, emotions, and values that intertwine in a complex web.

Consider the conflicts that arise within families – the friction between generations, the tug-of-war between siblings, and the delicate dance of spousal dynamics. These conflicts can be as subtle as disagreements over trivial matters or as profound as grappling with differing value systems.

Zooming out, we find conflicts embedded within the fabric of workplaces. Colleagues may clash over ideas, managers may struggle with employee performance, and teams may grapple with divergent goals. In the midst of these scenarios, the stakes can be high, impacting not only the individuals involved but also the overall productivity and atmosphere of the organization.

Venturing further into society, conflicts become entangled with socio-political issues. Communities grapple with differing ideologies, cultural clashes, and resource allocation disputes. These conflicts often carry historical baggage and are imbued with deeper meanings, making resolution all the more intricate.

The Dynamics of Conflict: A Kaleidoscope of Emotions

No matter the context, conflicts are driven by emotions, perceptions, and unmet needs. Anger, frustration, fear, and hurt are just a few of the emotions that can fuel conflicts. Understanding these emotional undercurrents is vital, as emotions can cloud judgment and hinder effective communication.

Moreover, conflicts are colored by power dynamics. In workplaces, authority figures may wield influence, while in families, parental roles can shape the tone of conflicts. Recognizing power imbalances and their effects on conflicts is essential for finding equitable solutions.

Cultural and Contextual Influences

The diversity of conflict scenarios is also shaped by cultural norms, societal expectations, and contextual factors. What may be considered acceptable conflict resolution in one setting might be viewed as confrontational in another. Cultural nuances impact communication styles, nonverbal cues, and the perceived appropriateness of certain strategies.

Additionally, the context within which conflicts occur plays a pivotal role. The urgency of a workplace conflict differs from that of an online disagreement, and the dynamics of resolving personal conflicts within an intimate relationship are distinct from those of addressing community-wide tensions.

The Path Forward: Adaptable Conflict Resolution

In embracing the diversity of conflict scenarios, it becomes evident that a one-size-fits-all approach to conflict resolution falls short. The key lies in adaptability – the ability to tailor strategies to fit the unique contours of each conflict. This book aims to equip you with a toolkit of conflict resolution techniques that can be applied across various settings, taking into account the emotional landscape, power dynamics, and cultural influences at play.

As we embark on this journey through the landscapes of conflicts, remember that conflicts, in their essence, are opportunities for growth, understanding, and positive change. By embracing this diversity and harnessing the lessons it offers, we position ourselves to become skilled conflict resolvers capable of navigating the intricate tapestry of conflicts that color our lives.

Adapting Conflict Resolution Strategies to Context

Conflict resolution is a dynamic process that requires a nuanced understanding of the context in which conflicts arise. A strategy that proves effective in one setting might yield different results in another due to the unique interplay of emotions, power dynamics, and cultural influences. As we embark on the journey of mastering conflict resolution, it's imperative to explore how to tailor our strategies to suit the intricacies of each context, ensuring that our efforts lead to constructive outcomes.

The Fluid Nature of Conflict Resolution Strategies

Just as conflicts take on various forms, so too do the strategies that address them. However, the effectiveness of a strategy isn't solely determined by its theoretical soundness; rather, it hinges on how well it's adapted to the context at hand. What might be a win-win solution in a workplace conflict might not be suitable for resolving tensions within an intimate relationship. Understanding this fluidity is the cornerstone of effective conflict resolution.

Mapping the Terrain: Analyzing Contextual Dynamics

Before diving into the strategies themselves, it's crucial to map out the contextual dynamics that shape the conflict. This involves identifying the key players, power dynamics, and emotions at play. In a workplace conflict, for example, recognizing the authority structures and the personalities of the individuals involved provides valuable insights that can guide strategy selection.

Cultural Considerations: Navigating Diversity

Cultural nuances significantly impact how conflicts are perceived and resolved. Different cultures place varying levels of emphasis on direct communication, individual versus collective needs, and hierarchical structures. Being attuned to these differences allows conflict resolvers to choose strategies that align with cultural expectations and promote understanding.

Choosing the Right Strategy: A Toolbox Approach

Rather than adopting a fixed approach to conflict resolution, consider building a toolbox of strategies that can be customized for each context. Some conflicts may benefit from a collaborative approach, while others might require assertive communication. The key is to recognize the strengths and limitations of each strategy and to apply them thoughtfully.

Strategies for Different Contexts

- Workplace Conflicts: In the workplace, strategies such as active listening, negotiation, and mediation can prove invaluable. Recognizing the hierarchical structure and the implications of conflicts on productivity guides the selection of strategies that balance individual needs with organizational goals.

- Family Dynamics and Relationships: Addressing family conflicts demands sensitivity to emotional ties and the power dynamics that exist within familial relationships. Strategies like empathy, open communication, and setting boundaries can facilitate healthy resolutions.

- Intimate Relationships and Partnerships: Conflicts within intimate relationships require an understanding of emotional intimacy, trust, and shared goals. Strategies like compromise, addressing underlying issues, and fostering emotional connection can mend rifts in these settings.

- Friendships and Social Circles: In social circles, preserving personal bonds is essential. Strategies such as active listening, finding common ground, and addressing misunderstandings directly contribute to maintaining healthy friendships.

- Communities and Societal Conflicts: For conflicts that span communities or societal divides, strategies such as dialogue facilitation, empathy, and collaborative problem-solving are effective in fostering understanding and addressing complex issues.

- Online Interactions: Digital conflicts call for strategies that counteract the challenges of online communication, including misinterpretation and anonymity. Strategies such as respectful communication, clarifying intentions, and disengagement from harmful interactions are paramount.

Conclusion: A Flexible Approach to Lasting Solutions

Adapting conflict resolution strategies to context is the key to achieving lasting solutions. As we explore the strategies tailored to each setting in the upcoming chapters, remember that adaptability, empathy, and open-mindedness are your allies in successfully navigating conflicts across the diverse landscapes of our lives. By mastering the art of adaptation, we become skilled conflict resolvers capable of transforming even the most complex scenarios into opportunities for growth and understanding.

Leveraging Your Skillset for Varied Situations

Conflict resolution is not a one-time skill to be mastered and then shelved; it's an evolving art that requires continuous refinement and adaptability. As we delve deeper into the realm of conflict resolution, it's essential to recognize that the skillset we develop can be harnessed across diverse situations. By honing these skills and learning how to apply them effectively, we position ourselves to navigate the complexities of conflicts, regardless of the setting they arise in.

The Core Conflict Resolution Skillset

At the heart of conflict resolution lie a set of foundational skills that serve as the building blocks for successful outcomes. These skills, though versatile, need to be tailored to the unique demands of each situation. Let's explore these skills and how they form the bedrock of our ability to address conflicts in any context.

- Active Listening: The ability to truly listen and understand the perspectives of others is a universal skill that underpins all conflict resolution efforts. By actively engaging with others' viewpoints, we demonstrate empathy and open the doors to effective communication.

- Empathy: Understanding and acknowledging the emotions and perspectives of those involved in a conflict is a fundamental step toward resolution. Empathy creates an environment where parties feel heard and valued, facilitating the process of finding common ground.

- Communication: Clear and effective communication is at the heart of conflict resolution. The skill of articulating thoughts and feelings, while also remaining open to others' input, is indispensable across all settings.

- Problem-Solving: Developing the ability to approach conflicts as shared challenges rather than competitions is a key aspect of effective conflict resolution. Problem-solving skills help identify common goals and paths toward resolution.

- Negotiation: Negotiation skills are vital for finding compromises and win-win solutions. These skills allow conflicting parties to balance their needs and work collaboratively toward resolution.

Adapting Skills to Varied Situations

Each setting introduces unique dynamics that require a tailored approach to conflict resolution. While the core skills remain consistent, their application and emphasis may differ. Let's explore how these skills can be leveraged in diverse situations:

Workplace Conflicts: In professional settings, active listening can help uncover underlying issues and concerns among colleagues. Empathy allows managers to understand their team's challenges, leading to more effective solutions. Effective communication becomes a bridge between hierarchical levels, fostering a positive and productive work environment.

Family Dynamics and Relationships: Empathy is paramount in familial conflicts, as understanding the emotional experiences of family members is key to resolution. Problem-solving skills help address complex family dynamics, while negotiation skills facilitate discussions about shared responsibilities and expectations.

Intimate Relationships and Partnerships: Communication and empathy are central to resolving conflicts within intimate relationships. Problem-solving skills guide discussions on issues like shared values, ensuring both partners' needs are addressed. Negotiation skills enable compromise without sacrificing the core of the relationship.

Friendships and Social Circles: Active listening and empathy strengthen the bonds of friendship by showing genuine care and concern. Communication skills help clarify misunderstandings, while negotiation skills aid in balancing individual preferences within the group.

Communities and Societal Conflicts: In community conflicts, active listening and empathy help bridge gaps between diverse perspectives. Effective communication allows for open dialogue, and problem-solving skills help address systemic issues. Negotiation skills play a role in bringing together conflicting groups toward common goals.

Online Interactions: Empathy is vital in digital conflicts, as it humanizes online interactions. Communication skills assist in interpreting tone and intent correctly, while problem-solving skills help find resolutions to online disputes. Negotiation skills allow for finding common ground and avoiding escalations.

Conclusion: Becoming a Versatile Conflict Resolver

As we explore conflict resolution strategies across varied scenarios, it's evident that the skills we cultivate are adaptable and powerful tools. By harnessing our ability to actively listen, empathize, communicate effectively, problem-solve, and negotiate, we become versatile conflict resolvers capable of addressing conflicts in any setting. This journey is not only about acquiring knowledge; it's about internalizing these skills and transforming them into a natural part of our approach to conflicts. In the chapters ahead, we will delve into these skills' application in different contexts, equipping ourselves to become masters of constructive conflict resolution across the diverse tapestry of our lives.

Chapter 1: Navigating Workplace Conflicts

Understanding Conflict Dynamics in the Workplace

Conflict is an intrinsic part of the workplace environment, arising from the convergence of diverse personalities, goals, and expectations. To effectively navigate workplace conflicts, it's essential to grasp the underlying dynamics that contribute to their emergence. By understanding the intricacies of conflict within professional settings, we can lay the groundwork for applying targeted conflict resolution strategies that foster collaboration and enhance productivity.

The Nature of Workplace Conflicts: A Multi-Faceted Lens

Workplace conflicts encompass a broad spectrum of situations, ranging from minor disagreements to more profound clashes of interest. These conflicts can emerge between colleagues, teams, or even between employees and management. At the core of these conflicts are often differing perspectives, goals, and communication breakdowns.

Sources of Workplace Conflict

1. Communication Breakdowns: Misunderstandings and misinterpretations can result from poor communication, leading to conflicts. Differences in communication styles, a

lack of clarity, or assumptions about intent can all contribute to this breakdown.

2. Power Dynamics: Hierarchical structures within organizations can create power imbalances that contribute to conflicts. Disagreements between managers and employees or tensions within teams can be exacerbated by these dynamics.

3. Competing Goals: Employees within the same organization may have differing priorities or objectives. When these goals clash, conflicts can arise as individuals vie for limited resources or recognition.

4. Interpersonal Differences: Conflicts may stem from personal differences in values, personalities, or work styles. These differences can lead to friction and affect collaboration.

5. Role Ambiguity: Unclear job roles and responsibilities can lead to overlaps or gaps, causing frustration and disputes among team members.

6. Organizational Change: Changes such as restructuring, mergers, or shifts in company culture can trigger conflicts as employees adapt to new circumstances.

The Emotional Landscape of Workplace Conflicts

Emotions play a pivotal role in workplace conflicts, often intensifying the issues at hand. Emotions such as frustration, resentment, and anger can cloud judgment and hinder productive communication. At the same time, emotions are valuable indicators of underlying concerns that need to be addressed.

Impact on Organizational Dynamics

Unresolved workplace conflicts can have far-reaching implications for organizations. They can lead to decreased employee morale, reduced productivity, increased absenteeism, and even talent loss through turnover. A toxic work environment driven by ongoing conflicts can erode trust and collaboration, hindering the organization's overall success.

Conclusion: Setting the Stage for Effective Conflict Resolution

Understanding the dynamics of workplace conflicts is the first step toward resolving them constructively. By recognizing the sources of conflicts, the emotional landscape they create, and their impact on organizational dynamics, we gain a comprehensive view of the challenges at hand. As we proceed through this chapter and the ones that follow, we will delve into strategies for addressing conflicts with colleagues, supervisors, and teams. Armed with insights into the nuances of workplace conflicts, we can develop a targeted approach that promotes open communication, empathy, and collaboration, fostering a harmonious and productive work environment.

Addressing Conflicts with Colleagues

Workplaces are dynamic ecosystems where a diverse array of personalities, skills, and ambitions converge. Inevitably, conflicts arise, stemming from differences in opinions, communication breakdowns, or competition for resources. Addressing conflicts with colleagues is a skill that holds immense value, as it contributes not only to a healthier work environment but also to increased collaboration and productivity. In this section, we will delve into the strategies and techniques that enable us to effectively address conflicts with colleagues, fostering understanding and constructive resolutions.

The Importance of Direct Communication

One of the foundational principles of resolving conflicts with colleagues is open and direct communication. Rather than allowing conflicts to fester under the surface, addressing them directly promotes transparency and ensures that issues are dealt with promptly. Effective communication requires active listening, where both parties can express their viewpoints without fear of judgment or interruption.

Recognizing Differing Perspectives

Conflicts often arise from differing perspectives on issues or projects. Acknowledging that there isn't always a single right answer and that multiple viewpoints can coexist is the first step toward resolution. Rather than approaching conflicts with the intention of proving one's own perspective, a collaborative mindset seeks to find common ground and explore mutually beneficial solutions.

Empathy as a Bridge to Resolution

Empathy is a powerful tool for resolving conflicts with colleagues. By putting ourselves in the other person's shoes, we gain insights into their motivations, concerns, and emotions. This understanding lays the foundation for more compassionate and effective communication. Expressing empathy demonstrates a genuine desire to comprehend the other person's viewpoint, fostering an atmosphere of respect.

Constructive Feedback: Balancing Honesty and Sensitivity

Giving and receiving feedback is an integral part of workplace dynamics, and it can be a source of conflict if not managed carefully. When addressing conflicts, providing constructive feedback requires a balance between honesty and sensitivity. Focus on the behavior or issue at hand rather than making personal attacks. Frame feedback in a way that encourages growth and improvement rather than criticism.

Conflict Resolution Techniques

1. Active Problem-Solving: Collaboratively addressing the core issue that led to the conflict is a proactive approach.

Identifying the root causes and brainstorming solutions allows both parties to work together toward resolution.

2. Mediation: If direct communication becomes challenging, involving a neutral third party as a mediator can provide a fresh perspective and facilitate a more productive discussion.

3. Seeking Common Ground: Identifying areas of agreement and shared goals can help bridge gaps and set the stage for productive collaboration.

4. Compromise: Sometimes conflicts require a middle ground where both parties make concessions. Compromise involves finding solutions that address each party's concerns to some extent.

5. Communication Enhancement: Improving communication methods, such as setting clear expectations, using non-confrontational language, and active listening, can prevent conflicts from escalating.

Navigating Power Dynamics

In addressing conflicts with colleagues, power dynamics can play a significant role. In cases where a colleague holds a position of authority, addressing the conflict can be challenging due to perceived repercussions. It's crucial to approach these situations with respect while advocating for open communication and resolution.

Conclusion: Fostering a Collaborative Workplace Culture

Addressing conflicts with colleagues is a skill that not only resolves immediate issues but contributes to a collaborative workplace culture. By embracing open communication, empathetic understanding, and effective conflict resolution techniques, we create an environment where conflicts are seen as opportunities for growth rather than obstacles. As we continue our exploration of conflict resolution in the workplace, we will delve into strategies for resolving conflicts with supervisors and managers, ultimately equipping ourselves with the tools to create harmonious and productive work relationships.

Resolving Conflicts with Supervisors and Managers" the sub topic for about 3000 words long

Conflict resolution within the workplace extends beyond interactions with colleagues; it also encompasses addressing conflicts with supervisors and managers. These conflicts can be particularly challenging due to the power dynamics at play. Effectively navigating conflicts with higher-ups requires a delicate balance of assertiveness, respect, and a strategic approach. In this section, we will explore strategies and techniques for resolving conflicts with supervisors and managers, ultimately fostering a healthy and constructive working relationship.

Understanding Power Dynamics

When conflicts involve supervisors or managers, power dynamics often come into play. These dynamics can create barriers to open communication, as employees may fear backlash or consequences for expressing their concerns. Recognizing these dynamics is essential for approaching conflicts with tact and consideration.

Approaching Conflicts with Respect

Addressing conflicts with supervisors and managers requires a respectful and professional demeanor. While open communication is crucial, it's essential to convey your viewpoint in a manner that reflects your commitment to your role and the organization's success. Avoid confrontational language and focus on the issue at hand rather than personal attacks.

Clarifying Expectations and Boundaries

Conflicts with higher-ups can sometimes arise from misunderstandings or vague expectations. Clarifying expectations and boundaries early on can prevent conflicts from escalating. Proactively seek opportunities to discuss your role, responsibilities, and objectives to ensure alignment and mitigate potential sources of conflict.

Using Constructive Feedback

Providing feedback to supervisors and managers can be delicate, but it's vital for growth and improvement. When offering feedback, focus on specific behaviors or situations rather than making generalized criticisms. Frame your feedback in a way that highlights your desire to contribute to a positive work environment and the overall success of the team.

Active Listening and Seeking Common Ground

When addressing conflicts with higher-ups, active listening is paramount. Understand their perspective and concerns before presenting your own. Seek common ground by identifying shared goals and interests. This approach builds a foundation for collaborative problem-solving and resolution.

Conflict Resolution Techniques

1. Scheduled Conversations: Request a private meeting to discuss the conflict at an appropriate time. Having a dedicated space for dialogue allows both parties to focus on the issue without distractions.

2. Framing the Conversation: Approach the conversation with a solution-oriented mindset. Present the conflict as an opportunity to enhance collaboration and contribute to the team's success.

3. Problem-Solving Together: Collaboratively identify the root causes of the conflict and brainstorm potential solutions. This approach demonstrates your commitment to working together for a positive outcome.

4. Mediation: If the conflict remains unresolved, consider involving a neutral third party or HR representative as a mediator. Their perspective can facilitate a more objective and productive discussion.

5. Documenting the Conversation: When discussing conflicts with higher-ups, consider taking notes or sending a follow-up email summarizing the conversation. This documentation can provide clarity and serve as a reference if needed in the future.

Assertiveness and Advocacy

Resolving conflicts with supervisors and managers often requires assertiveness while advocating for your viewpoint. Express your concerns and needs clearly, providing supporting evidence where necessary. Presenting well-reasoned arguments demonstrates your commitment to your role and the organization's success.

Balancing Respect and Self-Advocacy

Balancing respect for authority with self-advocacy is essential in conflict resolution with higher-ups. While expressing your viewpoint, acknowledge their perspective and the challenges they face as well. Demonstrating empathy and understanding creates an environment conducive to resolution.

Conclusion: Fostering Collaboration Across Hierarchies

Resolving conflicts with supervisors and managers is an integral part of creating a collaborative and productive work environment. By understanding power dynamics, using constructive communication techniques, and advocating for your viewpoint while maintaining respect, you contribute to an atmosphere where conflicts are addressed constructively. As we move forward in our exploration of workplace conflict resolution, we will delve into strategies for fostering harmonious team collaboration, equipping ourselves with tools to create a cohesive and effective work environment.

Strategies for Harmonious Team Collaboration

Team collaboration lies at the heart of a successful and productive workplace. When conflicts arise within teams, they can disrupt not only individual dynamics but also the overall group cohesion. Addressing conflicts and fostering harmonious team collaboration requires a combination of effective communication, shared goals, and a commitment to working together. In this section, we will explore strategies and techniques to promote harmonious collaboration within teams, enhancing productivity and synergy.

The Role of Effective Communication

Open and transparent communication is the cornerstone of harmonious team collaboration. Conflicts often arise from miscommunications or misunderstandings. By cultivating a culture of clear communication, teams can prevent conflicts from escalating and address them promptly when they do arise.

Establishing Team Norms and Guidelines

Teams can benefit from establishing norms and guidelines that outline expectations for communication, collaboration, and conflict resolution. These norms create a framework that guides interactions, ensures consistency, and promotes mutual respect.

Shared Goals and Alignment

A critical aspect of harmonious team collaboration is having shared goals and a shared sense of purpose. When team members are aligned around a common objective, conflicts are less likely to arise from divergent priorities. Collaboratively defining and refining goals encourages a sense of ownership and unity within the team.

Diversity as an Asset

Diverse teams bring a range of perspectives and ideas to the table. However, these differences can also contribute to conflicts. Embracing diversity as an asset involves valuing each team member's unique viewpoint and using it to enrich discussions and problem-solving.

Conflict Resolution Techniques for Teams

1. Regular Check-Ins: Schedule regular team check-ins to discuss ongoing projects, challenges, and potential conflicts. Creating a space for open dialogue helps prevent misunderstandings from festering.

2. Constructive Feedback Culture: Foster a culture of constructive feedback where team members feel comfortable offering and receiving input. This culture promotes continuous improvement and growth.

3. Clarify Roles and Responsibilities: Clearly define team members' roles and responsibilities to prevent overlaps

or gaps. When everyone understands their contributions, conflicts arising from role ambiguity can be minimized.

4. Mediation by a Leader: In situations where conflicts persist, team leaders or managers can serve as mediators. Their impartial perspective can help guide discussions toward resolution.

5. Team-Building Activities: Engage in team-building activities that foster trust and collaboration. These activities help team members understand each other's strengths, weaknesses, and communication styles.

Conflict Prevention Through Feedback

Regular feedback loops are instrumental in preventing conflicts within teams. Encouraging team members to provide feedback on processes, communication, and collaboration allows teams to adapt and improve continually.

Facilitating Collaborative Problem-Solving

When conflicts do arise within teams, adopting a problem-solving mindset can lead to productive outcomes. Encourage open dialogue where team members discuss their concerns and work together to identify potential solutions.

Building Emotional Intelligence

Emotional intelligence, the ability to understand and manage emotions, is crucial for harmonious team collaboration. Team members who are emotionally intelligent can navigate conflicts with empathy and maintain a positive team dynamic.

Conclusion: Cultivating Synergy Within Teams

Harmonious team collaboration is an art that involves nurturing open communication, shared goals, and a proactive approach to conflict resolution. By creating a supportive and respectful environment where diverse perspectives are valued, teams can harness their collective strengths to achieve outstanding results. As we continue to explore workplace conflict resolution, we will delve into strategies for unraveling family conflicts, addressing parent-child dynamics, and nurturing healthy relationships within extended families. These insights will contribute to our holistic understanding of conflict resolution across diverse settings.

Chapter 2: Family Dynamics and Relationships
Unraveling Family Conflicts: Roots and Patterns

Family is the crucible where our most intimate relationships are forged. While families can be a source of love and support, they are not immune to conflicts. Unraveling family conflicts involves delving into the complex interplay of emotions, histories, and dynamics that shape these conflicts. By understanding the roots and patterns of family conflicts, we can lay the groundwork for constructive resolution and nurturing healthier relationships.

The Complexity of Family Conflicts

Family conflicts are often multi-layered, stemming from a myriad of sources such as differences in values, misunderstandings, unresolved past issues, and even external stressors. These conflicts can span generations and involve extended family members, creating intricate webs that require careful examination.

Recognizing Patterns from the Past

Family conflicts are frequently rooted in patterns established over time. These patterns might arise from learned behaviors, unspoken expectations, or unresolved issues that are carried from one generation to the next. Recognizing these patterns is the first step toward breaking the cycle of recurring conflicts.

Communication Breakdowns

Miscommunication is a common catalyst for family conflicts. Within close relationships, assumptions about each other's intentions can lead to misunderstandings. This breakdown in communication can exacerbate conflicts and hinder resolution.

Unresolved Past Issues

Family conflicts often have deep historical roots. Past grievances, unaddressed hurts, and unresolved conflicts can resurface in new forms, fueling current disagreements. These unresolved issues highlight the importance of acknowledging and addressing past wounds.

Emotional Dynamics and Triggers

Families are fertile ground for emotional triggers, where even seemingly minor incidents can evoke intense reactions. These triggers are often linked to past experiences or family roles, and they can shape the way conflicts unfold.

Generational Influences

Generational values, beliefs, and cultural norms play a significant role in family conflicts. Understanding the generational differences that influence communication styles and expectations is key to resolving conflicts that arise from these disparities.

The Role of Sibling Dynamics

Sibling relationships are marked by their own unique dynamics, which can be both supportive and contentious. Birth order, competition for attention, and divergent life paths contribute to the complexities of sibling conflicts.

Breaking the Patterns of Family Conflicts

1. Open Communication: Establishing open and nonjudgmental communication channels within the family is crucial. Encourage family members to express their thoughts and feelings without fear of backlash.

2. Listening with Empathy: Empathetic listening is a powerful tool in family conflicts. Acknowledge each other's feelings and perspectives, demonstrating a genuine desire to understand.

3. Addressing the Past: To break patterns, families must address unresolved issues from the past. This requires a willingness to revisit painful memories and engage in healing conversations.

4. Seeking Professional Help: In cases where conflicts are deeply entrenched, seeking the guidance of a family therapist or counselor can provide an objective perspective and facilitate productive discussions.

5. Establishing Boundaries: Setting healthy boundaries within the family helps prevent conflicts from

escalating. Clear boundaries ensure that individual needs and preferences are respected.

Conclusion: Unraveling for Healing

Unraveling family conflicts involves peeling back layers to reveal the underlying emotions, patterns, and histories that contribute to discord. By addressing the root causes of conflicts and breaking free from repetitive patterns, families can embark on a journey of healing and growth. As we delve further into family dynamics, we will explore strategies for addressing parent-child conflicts constructively, fostering healthy sibling relationships, and nurturing bonds within extended families. This holistic exploration will equip us with the tools to navigate conflicts and foster harmonious relationships within our families.

Addressing Parent-Child Conflicts Constructively

Parent-child relationships are a cornerstone of family dynamics, shaping our emotional well-being and self-identity. While these relationships are built on love and care, conflicts between parents and children can be particularly intense due to differing expectations, generational gaps, and evolving roles. Addressing parent-child conflicts constructively is essential for fostering healthy communication, mutual understanding, and maintaining strong bonds. In this section, we will explore strategies and techniques for navigating parent-child conflicts in a way that promotes growth, empathy, and lasting harmony.

The Complexity of Parent-Child Conflicts

Parent-child conflicts arise from the natural process of differentiation, where children strive to establish their identities separate from their parents. These conflicts can stem from a range of issues, including differing values, life choices, personal boundaries, and the transition from dependency to independence.

Understanding Generational Shifts

Generational differences play a significant role in parent-child conflicts. Changing societal norms, technological advancements, and evolving cultural values can lead to disparities in expectations and communication styles between parents and their children.

The Parental Role in Conflict Resolution

Parents play a pivotal role in shaping the conflict resolution dynamics within the family. Modeling effective conflict resolution strategies and fostering an environment where open communication is encouraged can set the tone for healthier interactions.

Listening with Empathy

Empathetic listening is a cornerstone of addressing parent-child conflicts. Both parties should aim to truly understand each other's perspectives and emotions. Empathy creates a safe space for open dialogue, where feelings are acknowledged without judgment.

Separating Emotions from Issues

Parent-child conflicts can become emotionally charged, making it challenging to address the core issues. Separating emotions from the actual points of contention allows for a more focused and productive discussion.

Effective Communication Techniques

1. I-Statements: Encourage the use of "I" statements, where individuals express their feelings and concerns without placing blame. This fosters ownership of emotions and promotes open communication.

2. Active Listening: Active listening involves not only hearing the words being spoken but also understanding the emotions and intentions behind them. This technique promotes mutual understanding.

3. Timing and Setting: Choose a conducive time and setting for discussing conflicts. Avoid approaching discussions when either party is stressed, distracted, or in a rush.

4. Avoiding Defensiveness: Responding defensively can escalate conflicts. Instead, approach conflicts with an open mind, even if the conversation becomes uncomfortable.

Finding Common Ground

Identifying areas of agreement and shared values forms a foundation for resolving conflicts. Focusing on common ground allows parent and child to work together to find solutions that satisfy both parties' needs.

Negotiating Boundaries and Autonomy

Many parent-child conflicts arise from issues related to boundaries and autonomy. As children grow into adulthood, defining and respecting these boundaries is crucial. Parents must balance guidance with allowing their children the space to make their own decisions.

Seeking Professional Guidance

In cases where parent-child conflicts are deeply entrenched or emotionally charged, seeking the assistance of a family therapist or counselor can provide an impartial perspective and facilitate productive discussions.

Conclusion: Strengthening Bonds Through Resolution

Addressing parent-child conflicts constructively is an investment in the future of the relationship. By practicing effective communication, empathy, and finding common ground, both parents and children can navigate conflicts with respect and understanding. As we continue our exploration of family dynamics, we will delve into strategies for managing sibling rivalry, nurturing healthy relationships within extended families, and fostering a supportive family environment. This comprehensive understanding will equip us to create harmonious and resilient family relationships.

Sibling Rivalry and Conflict Resolution Strategies

Sibling relationships are a unique blend of companionship, camaraderie, and competition. Sibling rivalry, while a common phenomenon, can lead to conflicts that impact family dynamics. Addressing sibling rivalry and employing effective conflict resolution strategies is crucial for maintaining healthy sibling relationships, fostering mutual respect, and creating a supportive family environment. In this section, we will explore the dynamics of sibling rivalry, its underlying causes, and techniques to navigate conflicts constructively.

Understanding Sibling Rivalry

Sibling rivalry is a natural part of growing up in a family with multiple children. It encompasses a range of emotions, from jealousy and competition to loyalty and affection. While sibling rivalry can be healthy, excessive conflicts can strain relationships and negatively affect self-esteem.

Causes and Triggers

1. Attention and Affection: Sibling rivalry often arises from perceived inequalities in parental attention and affection. Children may compete for their parents' approval and love.

2. Birth Order: Birth order can influence sibling dynamics. Older siblings might feel a sense of responsibility, while younger ones may strive to establish their individuality.

3. Comparisons: Comparisons by parents or other family members can fuel competition and rivalry. Being labeled as "the smart one" or "the athletic one" can lead to tension.

4. Shared Resources: Conflicts over shared resources such as toys, personal space, and attention can escalate into rivalry if not managed properly.

The Role of Parenting

Parents play a significant role in either exacerbating or mitigating sibling rivalry. Strategies such as setting clear expectations, fostering equal attention, and addressing conflicts promptly can contribute to healthier sibling relationships.

Conflict Resolution Strategies

1. Promote Communication: Encourage open communication between siblings. Provide opportunities for them to express their feelings, frustrations, and concerns.

2. Teach Empathy: Help siblings understand each other's perspectives and emotions. Teaching empathy fosters compassion and reduces rivalry.

3. Neutral Mediation: As parents, act as neutral mediators in conflicts. Encourage siblings to express their viewpoints and guide them toward finding compromises.

4. Problem-Solving Together: Teach siblings to work together to find solutions to their conflicts. This collaborative approach helps them develop essential conflict resolution skills.

5. Individual Time: Dedicate individual time to each child to nurture their unique interests and strengths. This reduces the need for competition for parental attention.

Fostering Mutual Respect

Encouraging respect between siblings is essential for conflict resolution. This involves setting clear boundaries, emphasizing positive interactions, and modeling respectful behavior as parents.

Teaching Conflict Resolution Skills

Siblings can benefit from learning conflict resolution skills early in life. Teaching them active listening, compromise, and negotiation can equip them to manage conflicts constructively.

Celebrating Individuality

Recognize and celebrate each sibling's individual strengths and achievements. This reduces the need for comparison and minimizes rivalry.

Long-Term Effects of Constructive Conflict Resolution

Sibling relationships established through constructive conflict resolution strategies can have enduring positive effects. Siblings who learn to resolve conflicts respectfully are more likely to maintain strong bonds into adulthood.

Conclusion: Nurturing Lifelong Bonds

Addressing sibling rivalry and conflicts with effective strategies is an investment in nurturing lifelong bonds. By understanding the causes and triggers of sibling rivalry, promoting open communication, and fostering mutual respect, parents can create an environment where conflicts are opportunities for growth rather than sources of resentment. As we continue our exploration of family dynamics, we will delve into strategies for nurturing healthy relationships within extended families and fostering a supportive family environment. This holistic understanding will enable us to create harmonious and resilient family relationships.

Nurturing Healthy Relationships Within Extended Family

Extended families encompass a network of relationships that extend beyond the immediate household. These relationships can include grandparents, aunts, uncles, cousins, and in-laws. While extended families provide a sense of belonging and support, conflicts within these relationships can be intricate due to diverse personalities, generational gaps, and varying life experiences. Nurturing healthy relationships within the extended family requires understanding, empathy, and effective communication. In this section, we will delve into strategies and techniques for fostering harmonious connections and resolving conflicts within the extended family context.

The Diversity of Extended Family Dynamics

Extended families are a tapestry of experiences, traditions, and relationships. Conflicts within extended families can arise from differences in values, lifestyles, and expectations. Understanding and appreciating this diversity is key to building stronger connections.

Respecting Generational Differences

Generational differences within extended families can lead to misunderstandings and conflicts. Younger generations might embrace new technologies and lifestyles, while older generations value tradition and stability. Acknowledging these differences fosters mutual respect.

Embracing Cultural Diversity

In many extended families, cultural diversity is a defining aspect. Embracing different cultural backgrounds can enrich family experiences but can also contribute to misunderstandings. Emphasizing open dialogue about cultural norms and values promotes understanding.

Effective Communication Strategies

1. Regular Communication: Maintain regular communication with extended family members to stay connected and informed about each other's lives.

2. Active Listening: Practice active listening when interacting with extended family members. This demonstrates respect and understanding for their perspectives.

3. Clarifying Expectations: Clarify expectations when it comes to family gatherings, celebrations, and responsibilities. Clear communication reduces misunderstandings.

4. Resolving Conflicts Promptly: Address conflicts promptly rather than allowing them to fester. Open discussions prevent issues from escalating.

Fostering Shared Experiences

Creating opportunities for shared experiences can strengthen bonds within extended families. Gatherings, celebrations, and family traditions provide occasions to build connections and make lasting memories.

Respecting Boundaries

Understanding and respecting personal boundaries is crucial within extended families. Recognize that each individual's preferences and comfort zones may differ.

Navigating Conflicts Within Extended Families

1. Empathy and Understanding: Approach conflicts with extended family members with empathy and a willingness to understand their viewpoints and emotions.

2. Finding Common Ground: Identify shared values and interests to build connections and bridge gaps that may lead to conflicts.

3. Applying Constructive Communication: Use the same communication techniques you would with immediate family members, such as active listening and "I" statements.

4. Seeking Mediation: In cases where conflicts are complex, consider involving a neutral family member or seeking the assistance of a family therapist as a mediator.

Maintaining Boundaries in Decision-Making

Balancing individual decision-making with collective family decisions can be challenging. Extended family members should respect individual choices while also contributing to discussions.

Celebrating Individual Contributions

Acknowledge and celebrate the unique contributions and talents of each extended family member. This reinforces a sense of belonging and appreciation.

Conclusion: Cultivating Resilient Bonds

Nurturing healthy relationships within the extended family context requires an understanding of the diverse dynamics at play. By embracing generational differences, celebrating cultural diversity, and fostering effective communication, extended families can build resilient bonds that withstand conflicts and time. As we continue our exploration of family dynamics, we will delve into strategies for addressing conflicts in intimate relationships, resolving differences in value systems, and maintaining intimacy through conflicts. These insights will contribute to a holistic understanding of conflict resolution within various family settings, equipping us to navigate challenges and cultivate harmonious relationships.

Chapter 3: Intimate Relationships and Partnerships
Conflict's Role in Intimate Relationships

Intimate relationships are a tapestry woven with love, companionship, and shared experiences. However, conflicts are an inevitable part of this intricate weave. In fact, conflict can serve as a catalyst for growth, deeper understanding, and ultimately, stronger connections within intimate relationships. In this section, we will explore the multifaceted role of conflict in intimate relationships, understanding its sources, impact, and how constructive resolution can lead to transformative outcomes.

Conflict as a Natural Aspect of Intimacy

Conflict arises from the unique blend of personalities, backgrounds, and expectations that come together in an intimate relationship. Rather than fearing conflicts, couples can view them as opportunities for exploration and growth.

Understanding the Sources of Conflict

1. Communication Breakdowns: Misunderstandings, unspoken expectations, and differing communication styles can lead to conflicts.

2. Differing Values and Beliefs: Conflicts can emerge when partners hold differing values, beliefs, or life goals.

3. Unresolved Past Issues: Personal history and unresolved past conflicts can resurface and impact current disagreements.

4. Changing Dynamics: Transitions such as moving in together, having children, or career changes can introduce new stressors and potential conflicts.

Impact of Conflict on Intimate Relationships

1. Deeper Understanding: Conflicts provide an opportunity for partners to learn more about each other's perspectives, preferences, and emotions.

2. Increased Intimacy: Navigating conflicts together can lead to a heightened sense of intimacy as couples collaborate and support each other.

3. Resilience Building: Successfully resolving conflicts can strengthen a relationship's ability to withstand future challenges.

4. Learning and Growth: Conflicts encourage personal growth, self-awareness, and improved communication skills.

Negative Effects of Unresolved Conflicts

Unresolved conflicts can erode the foundation of intimacy within a relationship. They can lead to resentment, distance, and a breakdown in communication if not addressed promptly.

Conflict Resolution Strategies for Intimate Relationships

1. Embrace Open Communication: Create an environment where both partners feel safe to express their feelings and concerns openly.

2. Practice Active Listening: Listen attentively to each other's viewpoints without interrupting or formulating responses prematurely.

3. Use "I" Statements: Express feelings and concerns using "I" statements to avoid placing blame and encourage understanding.

4. Avoid Escalation: Stay focused on the issue at hand and avoid bringing up past grievances or unrelated topics that can escalate conflicts.

5. Take a Timeout: If a conflict becomes heated, consider taking a break to cool down before continuing the discussion.

Constructive Conflict Resolution

1. Seek Common Ground: Identify areas of agreement or shared goals that can serve as a foundation for resolution.

2. Collaborative Problem-Solving: Approach conflicts as joint challenges that you can solve together, rather than as a competition.

3. Apologize and Forgive: Apologizing and forgiving each other play a crucial role in moving past conflicts and healing emotional wounds.

4. Learn from Conflicts: Reflect on conflicts to understand their underlying causes and find ways to prevent similar issues in the future.

Professional Support

In some cases, conflicts within intimate relationships may require the guidance of a couples therapist or counselor. Seeking professional support can provide an objective perspective and offer strategies for effective communication and conflict resolution.

Conclusion: Strengthening Bonds Through Conflict

Conflict's role in intimate relationships is multifaceted. When approached constructively, conflicts can deepen understanding, enhance intimacy, and foster personal growth for both partners. By understanding the sources of conflicts, recognizing their impact, and employing effective resolution strategies, couples can navigate conflicts with respect, empathy, and the shared goal of strengthening their bond. As we continue our exploration of intimate relationships and partnerships, we will delve into addressing trust issues and jealousy, resolving conflicts arising from differing value systems, and strategies for maintaining intimacy through conflicts. These insights will contribute to a comprehensive understanding of conflict resolution in the context of intimate relationships, equipping us to create fulfilling and enduring partnerships.

Addressing Trust Issues and Jealousy

Trust is the cornerstone of intimate relationships, forming the foundation upon which love, vulnerability, and connection thrive. Yet, trust issues and jealousy can cast shadows on even the most loving partnerships. These emotions stem from insecurities, past experiences, and fears of betrayal. Addressing trust issues and jealousy in a relationship requires sensitivity, open communication, and a commitment to healing. In this section, we will explore the complexities of trust, the sources of jealousy, and strategies for navigating these challenges to strengthen the bond between partners.

Understanding Trust and Its Fragility

Trust is built over time through consistent reliability, honesty, and transparency. It's a delicate aspect of relationships that can be eroded by past betrayals, unmet expectations, or external influences.

Common Triggers of Trust Issues

1. Past Betrayals: Experiences of infidelity, lies, or broken promises can create lingering doubts and hinder the rebuilding of trust.

2. Insecurities: Individual insecurities about self-worth or fears of inadequacy can lead to mistrust in the relationship.

3. Lack of Communication: Misunderstandings arising from poor communication can give rise to suspicions and doubts.

4. External Influences: Factors such as social media, work-related interactions, or friendships can trigger feelings of jealousy and mistrust.

Understanding Jealousy

Jealousy is a complex emotion that can stem from feelings of insecurity, fear of abandonment, or a desire for exclusivity within the relationship.

Differentiating Between Healthy and Unhealthy Jealousy

Healthy jealousy involves expressing concerns in a constructive manner and seeking reassurance from one's partner. Unhealthy jealousy, on the other hand, can manifest as controlling behavior, possessiveness, or extreme emotional reactions.

Impact of Trust Issues and Jealousy

Trust issues and jealousy can create a cycle of negative emotions, strained communication, and distance between partners. If left unaddressed, they can lead to further mistrust and even the deterioration of the relationship.

Strategies for Addressing Trust Issues and Jealousy

1. Open Communication: Honest and transparent communication is vital for addressing trust issues. Partners should feel safe discussing their concerns and fears.

2. Active Listening: Both partners should actively listen to each other's perspectives without judgment, allowing space for vulnerability.

3. Exploring Triggers: Identifying the specific triggers of trust issues and jealousy can help partners understand the underlying emotions.

4. Rebuilding Trust: If trust has been compromised, both partners should work together to rebuild it through consistent actions, accountability, and understanding.

5. Set Boundaries: Establishing clear boundaries around interactions with others can help alleviate feelings of jealousy.

6. Seeking Professional Help: If trust issues and jealousy persist, seeking couples therapy can provide a safe space for addressing these challenges with the guidance of a trained professional.

Cultivating Self-Esteem and Self-Confidence

Individuals with higher levels of self-esteem and self-confidence are less prone to experiencing intense jealousy and mistrust. Partners can support each other's personal growth in these areas.

Encouraging Emotional Self-Awareness

Both partners should develop emotional self-awareness, understanding their triggers, and learning to manage their reactions to feelings of jealousy.

Creating a Supportive Environment

Partners should work together to create an environment of reassurance and emotional safety. This involves providing regular affirmations of love, commitment, and appreciation.

Conclusion: Nurturing Trust and Emotional Security

Addressing trust issues and jealousy requires a commitment to vulnerability, empathy, and open communication. By understanding the sources of these emotions, both partners can work together to create an environment of emotional security and reassurance. Trust can be rebuilt, and jealousy can be transformed into a catalyst for deeper self-awareness and growth. As we continue our exploration of intimate relationships and partnerships, we will delve into resolving conflicts arising from differing value systems, strategies for maintaining intimacy through conflicts, and navigating differing life goals. These insights will contribute to a comprehensive understanding of conflict resolution in the context of intimate relationships, enabling us to navigate challenges and foster enduring connections.

Conflict Resolution in Differing Value Systems

Intimate relationships are a merging of two unique individuals, each bringing their own set of values, beliefs, and perspectives. While these differences can enrich the partnership, they can also lead to conflicts rooted in differing value systems. Addressing conflicts arising from differing values requires empathy, open-mindedness, and effective communication. In this section, we will explore the complexities of navigating conflicts stemming from differing value systems, understanding their sources, and developing strategies to bridge these gaps while fostering mutual respect.

The Intersection of Value Systems

Value systems are deeply ingrained belief frameworks that shape our priorities, behaviors, and decisions. Conflicts can arise when partners hold conflicting values or prioritize different aspects of life.

Identifying Sources of Conflict

1. Cultural Backgrounds: Partners from diverse cultural backgrounds may have differing values related to family, relationships, and traditions.

2. Religious Beliefs: Religious differences can lead to conflicts in areas such as lifestyle choices, holidays, and child-rearing practices.

3. Career and Ambitions: Conflicting career aspirations or approaches to work-life balance can strain the partnership.

4. Family Dynamics: Disagreements about roles, responsibilities, and expectations within the family unit can lead to conflicts.

The Role of Open Communication

Effective communication is essential when conflicts arise from differing value systems. Partners must create a safe space to openly discuss their values, beliefs, and expectations.

Approaching Discussions with Empathy

Empathy is crucial for understanding each other's perspectives, even when they differ significantly. Partners should strive to empathize with the reasons behind their differences.

Conflict Resolution Strategies for Differing Value Systems

1. Focus on Understanding: Before seeking resolution, invest time in understanding each other's values and the reasons behind them.

2. Seek Common Ground: Identify shared values and goals that can serve as a foundation for compromise and resolution.

3. Find Middle Ground: In areas of conflicting values, seek middle ground that respects both partners' viewpoints.

4. Prioritize and Compromise: Prioritize which values are non-negotiable and be prepared to compromise in areas of lesser importance.

5. Create Flexible Solutions: Develop solutions that accommodate both partners' values, allowing for adaptability as circumstances change.

Balancing Individuality and Togetherness

Partners can maintain their individuality while also fostering a sense of togetherness. Finding a balance between shared values and personal beliefs is key.

Seeking External Perspectives

In cases of ongoing conflicts related to differing value systems, seeking advice from mentors, therapists, or counselors can provide impartial insights.

Personal Growth and Compromise

Both partners should be open to personal growth and change, acknowledging that their value systems may evolve over time.

Conclusion: Harmonizing Values for a Stronger Bond

Conflicts arising from differing value systems present an opportunity for growth, understanding, and deeper connection. By approaching these conflicts with empathy, open communication, and a commitment to compromise, partners can harmonize their values and build a stronger bond. The journey of resolving conflicts related to differing values requires patience, mutual respect, and a shared vision of creating a fulfilling partnership. As we continue our exploration of intimate relationships and partnerships, we will delve into strategies for maintaining intimacy through conflicts, applying conflict resolution to online interactions, and using conflict as a catalyst for positive societal change. These insights will contribute to a comprehensive understanding of conflict resolution in the context of intimate relationships, equipping us to navigate challenges and create lasting connections.

Strategies for Maintaining Intimacy Through Conflict

Intimacy in a relationship is not immune to the challenges of conflict. In fact, how partners navigate conflicts can significantly impact the depth of their intimacy. Maintaining intimacy through conflict requires a delicate balance of communication, emotional connection, and mutual understanding. In this section, we will explore strategies that can help couples preserve and even deepen their intimacy while addressing conflicts, fostering emotional closeness, and creating a resilient bond.

Understanding Intimacy in Relationships

Intimacy goes beyond physical connection; it encompasses emotional vulnerability, trust, and a sense of being deeply known by one's partner.

The Paradox of Conflict and Intimacy

While conflicts can strain intimacy, they also offer opportunities for partners to reveal their true selves, demonstrate care, and strengthen their connection.

Communication as the Key

Open and effective communication is the linchpin for maintaining intimacy through conflict. Partners should create an environment where they feel safe expressing their thoughts and feelings.

Embracing Vulnerability

Sharing vulnerabilities and fears during conflicts fosters emotional intimacy. Vulnerability encourages partners to connect on a deeper level and offer support.

Emotional First Aid

During conflicts, partners can provide emotional first aid by acknowledging each other's emotions and offering comfort. This strengthens emotional bonds and reinforces mutual care.

Strategies for Maintaining Intimacy Through Conflict

1. Stay Present: During conflicts, remain present and focused on the discussion. Avoid distractions that hinder effective communication.

2. Active Listening: Listen attentively to your partner's perspective, even if you disagree. Validate their feelings and let them know they are heard.

3. Avoid Blame: Replace blame with understanding. Focus on the issue at hand rather than attacking each other personally.

4. Use "We" Language: Frame conflicts as shared challenges that you'll tackle together. This promotes unity and partnership.

5. Express Appreciation: Regularly express appreciation for your partner's efforts, qualities, and

contributions. This reinforces a positive emotional connection.

Creating Shared Meaning

Intimate partners often share unique experiences, rituals, and traditions. These shared meanings contribute to a sense of unity and deepen the bond.

Prioritizing Quality Time

Amid conflicts, it's important to carve out quality time for each other. Engaging in shared activities and meaningful conversations nurtures the emotional connection.

Non-Verbal Communication

Non-verbal cues, such as physical touch, eye contact, and gestures of affection, play a significant role in maintaining intimacy during conflicts.

Resolving Conflicts Amicably

Conflicts can either draw partners closer or drive them apart. Choosing an amicable resolution paves the way for continued intimacy.

Reconnecting After Conflict

After a conflict, take time to reconnect emotionally. Engage in discussions that deepen your understanding of each other's viewpoints.

Seeking Professional Support

If conflicts become overwhelming, seeking couples therapy or counseling can provide a structured and supportive environment for addressing deeper issues.

Conclusion: Nurturing Intimacy Through Challenges

Conflict is an inherent part of relationships, but it need not diminish intimacy. In fact, when approached with care and intention, conflicts can strengthen the emotional connection between partners. By using open communication, vulnerability, and strategies for maintaining intimacy, couples can navigate conflicts while deepening their bond. As we continue our exploration of intimate relationships and partnerships, we will delve into addressing conflicts within friendships and social circles, promoting understanding in communities, and harnessing conflict as a catalyst for societal change. These insights will contribute to a comprehensive understanding of conflict resolution in the context of intimate relationships, equipping us to nurture enduring and fulfilling connections.

Chapter 4: Navigating Friendships and Social Circles

Handling Conflicts Among Friends

Friendships are valuable relationships that bring joy, support, and companionship to our lives. However, conflicts can arise even among the closest of friends. Navigating conflicts in friendships requires sensitivity, effective communication, and a commitment to understanding each other's perspectives. In this section, we will explore the dynamics of handling conflicts among friends, understanding the sources of disputes, and learning strategies to resolve conflicts while preserving the bond of friendship.

The Importance of Friendship

Friendships contribute to our emotional well-being and provide a sense of belonging. They offer companionship, shared experiences, and opportunities for personal growth.

Recognizing Common Sources of Conflict

1. Miscommunication: Misunderstandings and misinterpretations of words or actions can lead to conflicts among friends.

2. Unmet Expectations: Conflicts can arise when friends have differing expectations about the nature of the relationship or how it should evolve.

3. Jealousy and Envy: Feelings of jealousy or envy can create tensions among friends, particularly if one friend perceives the other as more successful or fortunate.

4. Personal Growth and Change: As individuals evolve, their values, interests, and priorities may shift, potentially leading to conflicts if not managed properly.

The Role of Open Communication

Clear and open communication is crucial when addressing conflicts among friends. Friends should feel comfortable discussing their feelings, concerns, and perspectives without fear of judgment.

Strategies for Handling Conflicts Among Friends

1. Choose the Right Time and Place: Pick an appropriate time and private setting to discuss the conflict, ensuring minimal distractions.

2. Express Yourself Honestly: Share your feelings and concerns honestly and respectfully, using "I" statements to avoid sounding accusatory.

3. Listen Actively: Allow your friend to express their viewpoint without interrupting. Show that you are genuinely interested in understanding their perspective.

4. Seek Understanding: Ask clarifying questions to ensure you fully understand your friend's point of view before responding.

5. Avoid Escalation: Stay focused on the specific issue at hand and avoid bringing up unrelated grievances that can escalate the conflict.

Fostering Empathy and Understanding

Put yourself in your friend's shoes to understand their emotions and motivations. This fosters empathy and helps in finding common ground.

Finding Compromises and Solutions

Approach conflicts as opportunities to find compromises that respect both friends' feelings and needs. Strive for win-win solutions.

Apologizing and Forgiving

Apologizing and forgiving are essential for resolving conflicts among friends. Owning up to mistakes and offering genuine apologies can mend hurt feelings.

Setting Boundaries

Clearly communicate boundaries and expectations within the friendship to avoid misunderstandings that can lead to conflicts.

Healing and Rebuilding Trust

If a conflict has strained the friendship, take steps to heal and rebuild trust. Consistent actions and open conversations are key.

Maintaining Boundaries in Group Settings

In group settings, conflicts among friends can be challenging to navigate. Focus on addressing conflicts privately to maintain the harmony of the group.

Conclusion: Strengthening Friendships Through Conflict

Conflicts within friendships are natural, but how we handle them determines the strength of the relationship. By using effective communication, empathy, and strategies for conflict resolution, friends can address disputes while preserving their bond. Friendship is a valuable connection worth nurturing, and resolving conflicts with care and understanding strengthens the foundation of trust and companionship. As we continue our exploration of navigating friendships and social circles, we will delve into managing group dynamics and conflicts, balancing personal boundaries and social connections, and strategies for strengthening bonds through constructive conflict resolution. These insights will contribute to a comprehensive understanding of conflict resolution in the context of friendships, equipping us to navigate challenges and create lasting and meaningful connections.

Managing Group Dynamics and Conflicts in Social Circles

In the realm of friendships and social circles, dynamics often expand beyond one-on-one relationships to encompass groups of individuals with varied personalities, interests, and perspectives. As the complexity increases, so does the potential for conflicts to arise within these group settings. Managing group dynamics and resolving conflicts in social circles requires a delicate blend of communication, empathy, and a commitment to maintaining harmonious relationships.

Understanding Group Dynamics

Social circles can range from close-knit friend groups to larger networks of acquaintances. Each group dynamic is unique, influenced by factors such as shared interests, personalities, and the power dynamics at play. Conflicts that emerge within these groups can stem from differences in opinions, competition for attention, or misunderstandings that ripple through multiple relationships.

Effective Communication and Active Listening

Open and effective communication is the cornerstone of managing group dynamics and conflicts. Ensuring that each member feels heard and understood promotes a sense of inclusion and prevents misunderstandings from escalating. Active listening becomes especially vital in larger group settings, where diverse viewpoints can contribute to more complex conflicts.

Mediating with Sensitivity

As conflicts unfold in social circles, it's crucial to approach mediation with sensitivity. Identifying a neutral mediator who can facilitate open discussions can help navigate the complexities of group dynamics. The mediator's role involves ensuring all voices are heard and steering conversations toward constructive solutions.

Creating Shared Norms and Boundaries

Establishing shared norms and boundaries within the social circle can help prevent conflicts from arising in the first place. Discussing acceptable behaviors, communication guidelines, and respectful interaction sets a foundation for healthy dynamics.

Respecting Individual Perspectives

In diverse social circles, varying perspectives are inevitable. Respecting these differences, even when conflicts arise, fosters an environment of inclusivity and growth. Encourage open discussions where differing viewpoints are acknowledged and addressed with respect.

Conclusion: Nurturing Harmony in Social Circles

Managing group dynamics and resolving conflicts in social circles is a dynamic process that demands effective communication, empathy, and a commitment to maintaining the bond between members. By understanding the unique dynamics at play, utilizing effective communication strategies, and respecting individual perspectives, social circles can transform conflicts into opportunities for growth, connection, and shared understanding. As we continue our exploration of navigating friendships and social circles, we will delve into balancing personal boundaries and social connections, strengthening bonds through constructive conflict resolution, and promoting understanding in communities. These insights will contribute to a comprehensive understanding of conflict resolution in various social contexts, equipping us to create enduring connections within our social circles.

Balancing Personal Boundaries and Social Connections

Finding the delicate equilibrium between personal boundaries and social connections is a fundamental aspect of maintaining healthy relationships within friendships and social circles. As individuals, we have unique needs, preferences, and limits, which must coexist with the desire for social interaction, companionship, and shared experiences. This section delves into the intricacies of achieving balance between personal boundaries and social connections, exploring the importance of self-care, open communication, and fostering a sense of belonging.

Understanding Personal Boundaries

Personal boundaries are the lines we draw to define our emotional, physical, and psychological limits. They are the crucial mechanisms that allow us to protect our well-being and maintain our autonomy within relationships.

The Spectrum of Social Connections

Social circles encompass a range of relationships, from close friendships to acquaintances. Managing personal boundaries becomes a nuanced task as we navigate relationships that vary in intimacy and frequency of interaction.

Importance of Open Communication

Clear and honest communication plays a pivotal role in balancing boundaries and connections. Articulating your boundaries to friends and acquaintances prevents misunderstandings and establishes mutual respect.

Self-Care as a Priority

Prioritizing self-care is essential in maintaining personal boundaries and sustaining healthy relationships. Recognizing when to step back, recharge, and assert your needs fosters overall well-being.

Creating a Sense of Belonging

Balancing boundaries doesn't equate to isolation; it's about forging meaningful connections without compromising personal well-being. Feeling a sense of belonging within a social circle is nurtured by a shared understanding and respect for each member's boundaries.

Conclusion: Navigating Boundaries for Fulfilling Connections

Balancing personal boundaries and social connections is a dance of self-awareness, empathy, and effective communication. Striking this equilibrium within friendships and social circles allows us to nurture fulfilling connections while safeguarding our individual well-being. By fostering an environment where personal boundaries are respected and valued, social circles can transform into spaces that enhance personal growth, shared experiences, and lasting connections. As we continue our exploration of navigating friendships and social circles, we will delve into strategies for strengthening bonds through constructive conflict resolution, promoting understanding in communities, and harnessing conflict as a catalyst for positive societal change. These insights will contribute to a comprehensive understanding of conflict resolution in various social contexts, equipping us to foster enduring connections within our social circles.

Strengthening Bonds Through Constructive Conflict Resolution

Conflict is not the antithesis of strong relationships; rather, it is an opportunity for growth, understanding, and the deepening of bonds. Friendships and social circles are no exception. Navigating conflicts in these contexts, when approached constructively, has the potential to enhance connections, reinforce trust, and create lasting bonds. This section explores the transformative power of using conflicts as stepping stones towards stronger relationships, emphasizing effective communication, empathy, and shared growth.

Conflict as a Catalyst for Growth

Conflicts in friendships and social circles can lead to greater self-awareness and insights into the dynamics of relationships. They prompt us to confront differences and vulnerabilities, enabling personal growth and the evolution of the relationship.

The Role of Effective Communication

Open and respectful communication is the cornerstone of turning conflicts into opportunities for strengthening bonds. Addressing issues directly and expressing feelings without blame fosters understanding and connection.

Building Empathy and Understanding

Conflict resolution is often a journey of empathizing with others' viewpoints. By placing ourselves in others' shoes, we gain insights into their feelings and motivations, fostering a deeper connection.

Finding Common Ground

In conflicts, there's potential to uncover shared values, goals, and aspirations. Identifying these commonalities can be a bridge toward resolving differences and reinforcing the foundation of the relationship.

Shared Problem-Solving

Approaching conflicts collaboratively fosters a sense of teamwork and unity within friendships and social circles. When everyone contributes to finding solutions, it reinforces the notion that challenges can be overcome together.

Conclusion: From Conflict to Connection

By harnessing the power of constructive conflict resolution, friendships and social circles can evolve into resilient networks of trust, support, and growth. Navigating conflicts with transparency, empathy, and shared problem-solving transforms adversity into a catalyst for deeper understanding and connection. The process teaches us that conflicts are not indicative of relationship frailty; rather, they are integral to the journey of building lasting and meaningful bonds. As we continue our exploration of navigating friendships and social circles, we will delve into promoting understanding in communities, applying conflict resolution to online interactions, and harnessing conflict as a catalyst for positive societal change. These insights will contribute to a comprehensive understanding of conflict resolution in various social contexts, equipping us to create enduring connections within our social circles.

Chapter 5: Promoting Understanding in Communities

Conflict in Diverse Community Settings

Communities are intricate tapestries of diverse individuals, each contributing unique perspectives, experiences, and backgrounds. With diversity comes the potential for conflicts to arise due to differing viewpoints, cultural nuances, and societal expectations. Navigating conflicts in diverse community settings requires a deep commitment to empathy, cultural sensitivity, and a shared goal of promoting understanding. This section delves into the complexities of conflict in diverse communities, emphasizing the importance of respectful dialogue, active listening, and fostering a sense of unity.

Understanding Diversity's Impact on Conflict

Diverse community settings encompass variations in culture, religion, ethnicity, socioeconomic status, and more. These differences can be sources of strength, but they can also lead to conflicts when misunderstandings arise due to differing norms and values.

Cultural Sensitivity and Empathy

Cultural sensitivity is paramount when addressing conflicts in diverse communities. Empathy and the ability to view conflicts from multiple cultural perspectives facilitate understanding and resolution.

The Role of Respectful Dialogue

Constructive conflict resolution in diverse communities hinges on open and respectful dialogue. Creating safe spaces for individuals to express their viewpoints fosters an environment where conflicts can be addressed without fear of backlash.

Active Listening as a Bridge

Active listening plays a pivotal role in promoting understanding in diverse communities. Attentively hearing others' experiences and concerns validates their perspectives and lays the foundation for productive discussions.

Fostering Unity Through Common Goals

Amid diverse viewpoints, focusing on shared goals that unite the community can bridge divides and redirect conflicts towards collaborative problem-solving.

Conclusion: Embracing Diversity for Harmony

Conflict in diverse community settings is an opportunity for growth and harmony. By approaching conflicts with cultural sensitivity, empathy, and an unwavering commitment to respectful dialogue, communities can transform conflicts into stepping stones for deeper understanding and unity. The process teaches us that diversity, far from being a source of division, can be a powerful catalyst for creating harmonious communities that value every voice and perspective. As we continue our exploration of promoting understanding in communities, we will delve into engaging in constructive dialogues with varied groups, addressing socio-political conflicts with empathy, and harnessing conflict as a catalyst for positive societal change. These insights will contribute to a comprehensive understanding of conflict resolution in diverse community contexts, equipping us to create inclusive spaces where conflicts are navigated with grace and the common goal of fostering understanding.

Engaging in Constructive Dialogues with Varied Groups

In diverse communities, conflicts often arise due to differing viewpoints, values, and cultural backgrounds. Engaging in constructive dialogues with varied groups is a powerful approach to address these conflicts and foster mutual understanding. These dialogues create spaces where individuals can share their perspectives, learn from one another, and work towards collaborative solutions. In this section, we delve into the art of engaging in productive dialogues with diverse groups, highlighting the significance of active listening, empathy, and the cultivation of shared goals.

The Importance of Dialogue in Diverse Communities

Dialogue serves as a bridge that connects individuals from different backgrounds, enabling them to exchange ideas and experiences. Constructive dialogues facilitate the exploration of diverse perspectives and provide opportunities for growth and change.

Active Listening as the Foundation

Active listening is the cornerstone of effective dialogue. When individuals listen attentively to others' viewpoints, they demonstrate respect and create an environment conducive to open communication.

Fostering Empathy and Understanding

Empathy is a driving force in promoting understanding. By putting themselves in others' shoes, individuals can better grasp the emotions and motivations behind different viewpoints, breaking down barriers to communication.

Creating Safe Spaces for Dialogue

Establishing safe spaces is essential for fostering productive conversations. Participants should feel secure in sharing their thoughts without fear of judgment or reprisal.

Seeking Common Ground and Shared Goals

Engaging in dialogue is not about convincing others to change their views. Instead, it's about finding common ground and shared goals that allow diverse groups to work together for positive change.

Conclusion: Dialogue as a Catalyst for Change

Engaging in constructive dialogues with varied groups is an instrument of change in diverse communities. It enables individuals to transcend biases, embrace diverse perspectives, and forge connections based on mutual respect. Through dialogue, conflicts can be transformed into opportunities for growth, learning, and collaborative problem-solving. As we continue our exploration of promoting understanding in communities, we will delve into addressing socio-political conflicts with empathy, harnessing conflict as a catalyst for positive societal change, and advocating for social justice through conflict resolution. These insights will contribute to a comprehensive understanding of conflict resolution in diverse community contexts, equipping us to engage in meaningful dialogues that bridge divides and cultivate a culture of unity and understanding.

Addressing Socio-Political Conflicts with Empathy

Socio-political conflicts within communities can be some of the most challenging to navigate due to the deeply entrenched beliefs and emotions they evoke. However, addressing these conflicts with empathy can be a transformative approach to promote understanding and bridge divides. This section delves into the complexities of addressing socio-political conflicts with empathy, highlighting the importance of active listening, perspective-taking, and cultivating a shared commitment to positive change.

The Nuances of Socio-Political Conflicts

Socio-political conflicts often stem from differing ideologies, beliefs, and societal perspectives. These conflicts can be polarizing, creating divisions that hinder progress and harmony within communities.

The Role of Empathy in Conflict Resolution

Empathy is a potent tool in addressing socio-political conflicts. By genuinely attempting to understand the emotions and experiences of others, individuals can transcend their own biases and open the door to meaningful dialogue.

Active Listening and Open-Mindedness

Active listening involves not only hearing the words spoken but also grasping the underlying emotions and motivations. In socio-political conflicts, active listening paves the way for respectful conversations that go beyond surface-level disagreements.

Perspective-Taking for Deeper Understanding

Putting oneself in another's shoes is a key step in addressing socio-political conflicts. Perspective-taking allows individuals to acknowledge the reasons behind different viewpoints, fostering empathy and connection.

Cultivating a Shared Commitment to Change

In socio-political conflicts, the common goal should be positive change for the betterment of the community. By shifting the focus from winning arguments to creating meaningful change, individuals can find common ground.

Conclusion: Empathy as a Path to Unity

Addressing socio-political conflicts with empathy is a courageous step towards unity and understanding. Empathy breaks down barriers, opens lines of communication, and challenges individuals to transcend their preconceived notions. By engaging in empathetic conversations, communities can work towards reconciliation, shared growth, and a brighter future. As we continue our exploration of promoting understanding in communities, we will delve into harnessing conflict as a catalyst for positive societal change, advocating for social justice through conflict resolution, and collaborative efforts for change in larger societal conflicts. These insights will contribute to a comprehensive understanding of conflict resolution in diverse community contexts, equipping us to navigate the complexities of socio-political conflicts with empathy and a shared commitment to fostering positive change.

Fostering Harmony in Local and Global Communities

Creating harmony within both local and global communities requires a proactive commitment to conflict resolution and the cultivation of shared values. Communities, whether on a local or global scale, are composed of diverse individuals, each bringing their unique perspectives and experiences. Fostering understanding and unity within these communities involves a blend of effective communication, collaboration, and a shared vision for positive change. This section explores the intricacies of promoting harmony in communities, emphasizing the significance of empathy, cross-cultural engagement, and collaborative efforts for change.

Understanding Local and Global Community Dynamics

Local communities are the microcosms in which we live, while global communities transcend geographical boundaries through shared interests, goals, and causes. Both contexts harbor opportunities for connection and growth, but they also present challenges that require adept conflict resolution.

Empathy as a Bridge

Empathy serves as a bridge that spans differences and connects individuals from various walks of life. Fostering harmony in communities begins with understanding the emotions and experiences of others, creating a foundation for mutual respect.

Cross-Cultural Engagement and Learning

In a globalized world, communities are increasingly multicultural. Engaging with individuals from different cultures broadens perspectives and dispels stereotypes, creating a platform for open dialogue and harmonious coexistence.

Collaborative Efforts for Positive Change

Communities thrive when members collaborate to address shared challenges. Collaborative initiatives harness the collective strength of diverse voices, channeling conflict resolution towards positive change and growth.

Promoting a Sense of Shared Identity

Fostering harmony often involves nurturing a shared sense of identity based on common values and aspirations. This shared identity transcends differences and unites community members in their pursuit of a better future.

Conclusion: The Power of Harmony in Communities

Fostering harmony within local and global communities is an endeavor that requires dedication, empathy, and a shared commitment to positive change. By engaging in empathetic conversations, cross-cultural engagement, and collaborative efforts, communities can transcend conflicts and create spaces where understanding and unity prevail. As we conclude our exploration of promoting understanding in communities, we have journeyed through the intricacies of addressing socio-political conflicts with empathy, harnessing conflict as a catalyst for positive change, advocating for social justice through conflict resolution, and collaborative efforts for change in larger societal conflicts. These insights contribute to a comprehensive understanding of conflict resolution in diverse community contexts, equipping us to navigate the challenges of fostering harmony in communities both near and far.

Chapter 6: Applying Conflict Resolution to Online Interactions

Navigating Conflicts in the Digital Age

The digital age has revolutionized the way we communicate, connect, and interact with others. While online platforms offer unprecedented opportunities for global engagement and discourse, they also introduce new challenges and complexities when it comes to conflict resolution. Navigating conflicts in the digital age demands a unique set of skills and strategies that are grounded in empathy, effective communication, and a nuanced understanding of online dynamics. This section delves into the intricacies of addressing conflicts in online interactions, highlighting the importance of digital etiquette, understanding the virtual environment, and cultivating constructive conversations.

The Digital Landscape: An Evolution of Interaction

The rise of social media, forums, and online communities has reshaped how we engage with one another. These platforms offer spaces for communication, expression, and sharing, but they also magnify the potential for misunderstandings and conflicts due to the absence of non-verbal cues and the anonymity they provide.

Challenges of Online Conflict Resolution

Conflicts in the digital realm are unique due to the barrier of screens and the speed at which communication occurs. Misinterpretations, miscommunications, and the ease of spreading information can amplify conflicts if not addressed effectively.

Digital Etiquette: A Foundation for Online Interactions

Establishing and adhering to digital etiquette is crucial for maintaining respectful online interactions. Tone, language, and the choice of words play pivotal roles in preventing conflicts and promoting healthy conversations.

Empathy in the Digital World

Empathy is equally important online as it is offline. Recognizing that behind each username or profile picture is a real person with emotions and experiences fosters a sense of understanding and promotes a more empathetic approach to conflict resolution.

Cultivating Constructive Conversations

Navigating conflicts in the digital age requires skills in steering conversations away from toxicity and towards constructive engagement. Asking clarifying questions, avoiding personal attacks, and focusing on the issue at hand are key strategies.

Conclusion: The Art of Resolving Conflicts Online

Addressing conflicts in the digital age is an art that requires adapting traditional conflict resolution techniques to the nuances of the virtual environment. By recognizing the unique challenges of online interactions, practicing digital etiquette, and approaching conflicts with empathy and constructive intent, we can navigate the digital landscape with a commitment to fostering understanding, even in the face of differing opinions and perspectives. As we continue our exploration of applying conflict resolution to online interactions, we will delve into resolving misunderstandings in virtual communication, addressing online bullying and harassment, and promoting positive interactions in online communities. These insights will contribute to a comprehensive understanding of conflict resolution in the digital age, equipping us to navigate conflicts with grace and civility in the ever-evolving online world.

Resolving Misunderstandings in Virtual Communication

Virtual communication has become a cornerstone of modern interaction, offering convenience and immediacy. However, the absence of nonverbal cues and the reliance on text can lead to misunderstandings and conflicts. Resolving these misunderstandings requires a combination of effective communication skills, active listening, and the ability to navigate the limitations of the digital medium. This section delves into the complexities of addressing misunderstandings in virtual communication, emphasizing the importance of clear communication, empathy, and fostering a culture of open dialogue.

Understanding the Dynamics of Virtual Communication

In virtual communication, nuances like tone, facial expressions, and body language are absent. Text-based conversations can easily be misconstrued, leading to unintended misunderstandings that, if left unresolved, can escalate into conflicts.

The Role of Effective Communication

Effective communication is a linchpin in preventing and resolving misunderstandings online. Articulating thoughts clearly and concisely reduces the likelihood of misinterpretation and promotes understanding.

Active Listening in the Digital Realm

Active listening extends to virtual communication as well. By reading messages thoroughly, seeking clarification, and acknowledging the emotions behind the words, individuals can validate each other's perspectives and address misunderstandings promptly.

The Power of Empathy in Virtual Contexts

Empathy plays a pivotal role in resolving misunderstandings online. By imagining the emotions and intentions behind messages, individuals can foster a sense of connection that mitigates misinterpretation and promotes open communication.

Fostering a Culture of Open Dialogue

Creating an environment where individuals feel comfortable addressing misunderstandings encourages open dialogue. This requires a collective commitment to clear communication, respectful exchanges, and a willingness to resolve conflicts amicably.

Conclusion: Bridging Gaps in Virtual Spaces

Addressing misunderstandings in virtual communication requires a unique set of skills that combine traditional conflict resolution principles with an understanding of the digital landscape. By embracing effective communication techniques, practicing active listening, and approaching conflicts with empathy and open-mindedness, individuals can bridge gaps, prevent escalations, and foster a culture of understanding in the digital realm. As we continue our exploration of applying conflict resolution to online interactions, we will delve into addressing online bullying and harassment, promoting positive interactions in online communities, and harnessing the potential of digital platforms for constructive dialogue. These insights will contribute to a comprehensive understanding of conflict resolution in the digital age, equipping us to navigate misunderstandings with finesse and promote harmony in virtual spaces.

Addressing Online Bullying and Harassment

As online interactions become more prevalent, so too does the unfortunate rise of online bullying and harassment. These harmful behaviors can lead to emotional distress, social isolation, and even real-world consequences for victims. Addressing online bullying and harassment requires a multifaceted approach that involves understanding the dynamics of cyberbullying, promoting digital empathy, and advocating for a safer online environment. This section delves into the complexities of tackling online bullying and harassment, emphasizing the importance of awareness, intervention strategies, and fostering a culture of respect.

Understanding Online Bullying and Harassment

Online bullying and harassment involve the intentional use of digital platforms to target and harm individuals. It encompasses a range of behaviors, from hurtful comments and personal attacks to sharing private information without consent.

The Psychological Impact of Cyberbullying

The effects of online bullying can be deeply profound, leading to feelings of anxiety, depression, and low self-esteem. Victims often grapple with isolation and emotional turmoil.

Promoting Digital Empathy and Respect

Cultivating empathy in the digital realm is pivotal in preventing online bullying. Encouraging users to treat others with the same respect and consideration they would in face-to-face interactions contributes to a more compassionate online environment.

Intervention Strategies

Effective intervention strategies play a crucial role in addressing online bullying and harassment. Reporting mechanisms, moderation, and educating users about the consequences of their actions can deter harmful behavior.

Creating a Safer Online Environment

Online platforms and communities bear the responsibility of creating a safe space for users. Implementing strict anti-bullying policies, robust reporting mechanisms, and proactive moderation can contribute to curbing online harassment.

Conclusion: Nurturing Digital Empathy and Safety

Addressing online bullying and harassment requires vigilance, education, and a collective commitment to promoting digital empathy. By understanding the dynamics of cyberbullying, intervening effectively, and fostering a culture of respect and responsibility, we can work towards a safer and more inclusive online environment. As we conclude our exploration of applying conflict resolution to online interactions, we have journeyed through the complexities of resolving misunderstandings in virtual communication, addressing online bullying and harassment, promoting positive interactions in online communities, and harnessing the potential of digital platforms for constructive dialogue. These insights contribute to a comprehensive understanding of conflict resolution in the digital age, equipping us to navigate the challenges of promoting harmony and empathy in virtual spaces.

Promoting Positive Interactions in Online Communities

Online communities have transformed the way we connect and share information, offering spaces for collaboration, support, and discourse. However, maintaining a positive and constructive atmosphere within these communities is essential to foster healthy interactions and prevent conflicts. Promoting positive interactions in online communities involves cultivating digital citizenship, encouraging respectful dialogue, and establishing norms that prioritize empathy and understanding. This section delves into the intricacies of creating a positive online environment, emphasizing the importance of community guidelines, moderating effectively, and nurturing a sense of belonging.

The Power of Online Communities

Online communities encompass a vast array of interests and topics, uniting individuals across geographical boundaries. These communities facilitate the exchange of knowledge, experiences, and support, but they can also be susceptible to negativity and conflicts.

Cultivating Digital Citizenship

Promoting positive interactions starts with cultivating digital citizenship. Encouraging users to be responsible, respectful, and ethical in their online behavior lays the foundation for a harmonious community.

The Role of Community Guidelines

Clear and comprehensive community guidelines provide users with a framework for appropriate behavior. These guidelines communicate expectations, outline consequences for misconduct, and promote a sense of accountability.

Encouraging Respectful Dialogue

Respectful dialogue is the cornerstone of positive interactions. Encouraging users to engage in civil conversations, consider diverse viewpoints, and refrain from personal attacks enhances the quality of discussions and prevents conflicts.

Effective Community Moderation

Effective moderation is crucial for maintaining a positive online environment. Moderators play a pivotal role in enforcing guidelines, addressing conflicts promptly, and creating a safe space for users to express themselves.

Nurturing a Sense of Belonging

Online communities thrive when users feel a sense of belonging. Fostering connections, acknowledging contributions, and valuing diverse voices contribute to a culture of inclusivity and positivity.

Conclusion: Building Digital Bridges

Promoting positive interactions in online communities requires a concerted effort from both users and community administrators. By embracing the principles of digital citizenship, adhering to community guidelines, and engaging in respectful dialogue, individuals can collectively build digital bridges that foster meaningful connections and knowledge-sharing. As we conclude our exploration of applying conflict resolution to online interactions, we have traversed the complexities of resolving misunderstandings in virtual communication, addressing online bullying and harassment, promoting positive interactions in online communities, and harnessing the potential of digital platforms for constructive dialogue. These insights contribute to a comprehensive understanding of conflict resolution in the digital age, equipping us to navigate the digital landscape with empathy, respect, and a commitment to nurturing positive interactions.

Chapter 7: Conflict as Catalyst for Societal Change
Harnessing Conflict for Positive Transformation

Conflict is often viewed through a negative lens, associated with discord and disruption. However, conflict also possesses the potential to be a catalyst for positive transformation on both individual and societal levels. When harnessed constructively, conflicts can drive change, challenge unjust systems, and inspire growth. This section explores the transformative power of conflict as a driver for positive societal change, emphasizing the importance of recognizing conflict's potential, reframing perceptions, and embracing discomfort to create a more just and equitable world.

Redefining Conflict: A Catalyst for Change

To harness conflict for positive transformation, we must first shift our perception of it. Conflict can be seen as a natural outcome of differing perspectives, and its energy can be directed towards positive ends.

Embracing Discomfort for Growth

Positive transformation often emerges from discomfort. By leaning into challenging conversations and situations, individuals and societies can confront ingrained biases and outdated norms.

Conflict and Social Justice

Conflict can be a powerful force in challenging systemic injustices. Movements for civil rights, gender equality, and environmental sustainability have been fueled by the conflict between marginalized voices and dominant power structures.

Fostering Constructive Dialogue

Constructive dialogue is key to harnessing conflict for change. Engaging in respectful conversations that encourage critical thinking and active listening allows conflicting perspectives to coexist and evolve.

Nurturing Collaborative Efforts

Positive transformation requires collaborative efforts. When individuals and groups with conflicting viewpoints come together to address shared challenges, the potential for innovative solutions and societal change is amplified.

Conclusion: Conflict as a Catalyst for a Better Future

Harnessing conflict for positive transformation requires a collective commitment to dialogue, growth, and societal betterment. By reframing conflict, embracing discomfort, advocating for social justice, fostering constructive dialogue, and nurturing collaborative efforts, we can channel conflict's energy towards creating a more equitable and just world. As we conclude our exploration of conflict as a catalyst for societal change, we have journeyed through the depths of advocating for social justice through conflict resolution, collaborative efforts for change in larger societal conflicts, and using lessons from conflict to shape a more equitable future. These insights contribute to a comprehensive understanding of conflict's potential to drive positive transformation, equipping us to navigate conflicts with a purpose and contribute to the ongoing journey of shaping a better world for all.

Advocating for Social Justice through Conflict Resolution

Conflict and social justice are interconnected in a profound way. As conflicts arise from the clash of differing values, perspectives, and interests, they often shed light on systemic inequalities and injustices within societies. Advocating for social justice through conflict resolution involves harnessing conflict's energy to challenge oppressive systems, amplify marginalized voices, and drive transformative change. This section delves into the powerful role conflict resolution plays in advocating for social justice, emphasizing the importance of awareness, allyship, intersectionality, and creating inclusive spaces for dialogue.

Understanding the Link between Conflict and Social Justice

Conflicts can illuminate disparities in power and privilege that perpetuate social injustices. The tension between opposing forces can expose deep-seated inequalities that demand examination and transformation.

The Power of Conflict to Drive Change

Conflict serves as a wake-up call, urging society to confront its shortcomings. The discomfort that accompanies conflicts can propel individuals and communities to demand equitable change.

Amplifying Marginalized Voices

Conflict resolution creates platforms for marginalized voices to be heard. By providing spaces for open dialogue, conflicts give voice to those who have been historically silenced.

Allyship and Solidarity in Conflict Resolution

Advocating for social justice requires allyship and solidarity. Those in positions of privilege must engage in conflict resolution to stand up against discrimination and amplify the voices of marginalized groups.

Intersectionality: Recognizing Complex Identities

Conflict resolution for social justice must acknowledge intersectionality—the interconnected nature of social identities. Understanding how various aspects of an individual's identity intersect can lead to more nuanced and inclusive solutions.

Creating Inclusive Spaces for Dialogue

Inclusive dialogue spaces are essential for advocating for social justice. By creating environments where individuals from diverse backgrounds can share their experiences and perspectives, conflicts can lead to greater understanding and change.

Conclusion: Conflict Resolution as a Tool for Change

Advocating for social justice through conflict resolution is an act of courage and empathy. By recognizing the link between conflict and systemic injustices, amplifying marginalized voices, practicing allyship, acknowledging intersectionality, and creating inclusive dialogue spaces, we can harness conflict's potential to drive transformative change. As we conclude our exploration of conflict as a catalyst for societal change, we have journeyed through the depths of harnessing conflict for positive transformation, collaborative efforts for change in larger societal conflicts, and using lessons from conflict to shape a more equitable future. These insights contribute to a comprehensive understanding of conflict's role in advocating for social justice, equipping us to navigate conflicts with a purpose and contribute to the ongoing journey of building a more just and inclusive society for all.

Collaborative Efforts for Change in Larger Societal Conflicts

Societal conflicts can be vast and deeply entrenched, often involving complex issues such as systemic oppression, human rights violations, and political upheaval. Addressing these conflicts requires collaborative efforts that bring together individuals, communities, and organizations to drive meaningful change. Collaborative efforts for change in larger societal conflicts involve coalition-building, strategic advocacy, and the cultivation of collective impact. This section delves into the intricate process of effecting change in larger societal conflicts, emphasizing the importance of shared goals, diverse perspectives, and sustained engagement.

The Complexity of Societal Conflicts

Larger societal conflicts are rooted in historical, cultural, and structural factors. These conflicts often impact the lives of countless individuals and necessitate multi-faceted approaches.

Building Coalitions for Collective Action

Collaborative efforts begin with building coalitions. Bringing together diverse stakeholders who share a common goal amplifies voices, resources, and impact.

Strategic Advocacy for Systemic Change

Societal conflicts require strategic advocacy that targets systemic issues. Advocates work to influence policies, laws, and institutional practices that perpetuate injustice.

The Power of Collective Impact

Collective impact is about aligning efforts for maximum effect. When individuals and organizations collaborate, their combined strength has the potential to drive transformative change.

Navigating Differences and Disagreements

Collaborative efforts involve individuals with differing perspectives. Navigating these differences requires open dialogue, active listening, and a shared commitment to the greater good.

Sustaining Engagement for Long-Term Impact

Creating change in larger societal conflicts is a marathon, not a sprint. Sustained engagement, ongoing dialogue, and adaptability are essential to see long-lasting transformation.

Conclusion: Unity in Diversity for Societal Change

Collaborative efforts for change in larger societal conflicts embody the power of unity in diversity. By building coalitions, advocating strategically, harnessing collective impact, navigating disagreements, and sustaining engagement, individuals and communities can create a ripple effect that challenges the roots of societal conflicts. As we conclude our exploration of conflict as a catalyst for societal change, we have journeyed through the depths of harnessing conflict for positive transformation, advocating for social justice through conflict resolution, and using lessons from conflict to shape a more equitable future. These insights contribute to a comprehensive understanding of collaborative efforts for change in larger societal conflicts, equipping us to navigate these challenges with determination and unity, and work towards a more just and harmonious society for all.

Using Lessons from Conflict to Shape a More Equitable Future

Conflicts, whether personal or societal, offer valuable insights that can guide us towards a more equitable and just future. By reflecting on the lessons learned from conflicts, we can identify patterns, challenge existing norms, and work towards systemic change. Using lessons from conflict to shape a more equitable future involves a commitment to learning, introspection, and actively applying those lessons to create positive transformation. This section delves into the transformative potential of conflict-derived insights, emphasizing the importance of self-awareness, critical analysis, and sustained action.

Learning from Conflict: A Path to Growth

Conflict is a teacher that reveals hidden truths about ourselves and society. Embracing conflicts as learning opportunities allows us to evolve and contribute to positive change.

Personal Growth and Self-Reflection

Conflicts prompt us to reflect on our behaviors, biases, and values. Self-awareness gained through conflict can lead to personal growth and a deeper understanding of our impact on others.

Identifying Systemic Injustices

Conflicts often expose systemic inequalities and injustices. Analyzing the root causes of conflicts can reveal structural issues that need to be addressed for lasting change.

Transcending Polarization and Division

Learning from conflict encourages us to transcend polarization and seek common ground. Conflict-derived insights can guide us in finding shared values and building bridges.

Applying Conflict-Resolution Strategies to Everyday Life

Conflict-resolution strategies learned from addressing conflicts can be applied to everyday life. Active listening, empathy, and effective communication enhance relationships and promote understanding.

Sustaining the Momentum for Change

Using lessons from conflict to shape a more equitable future requires sustained effort. Advocacy, allyship, and continuous learning are essential to maintain momentum and effect lasting change.

Conclusion: Forging a New Path through Conflict's Wisdom

Using lessons from conflict is an intentional choice to shape a more equitable and just future. By learning from conflicts, embracing personal growth, identifying systemic issues, transcending divisions, applying conflict-resolution strategies, and sustaining the momentum for change, we can navigate conflicts with purpose and contribute to a transformative journey. As we conclude our exploration of conflict as a catalyst for societal change, we have journeyed through the depths of harnessing conflict for positive transformation, advocating for social justice through conflict resolution, collaborative efforts for change in larger societal conflicts, and using lessons from conflict to shape a more equitable future. These insights contribute to a comprehensive understanding of how lessons from conflict can pave the way towards a brighter future, equipping us to navigate conflicts with wisdom and contribute to the ongoing journey of building a more just and equitable society for all.

Conclusion
Reflecting on the Diversity of Conflict Resolution Challenges

Throughout this exploration of conflict resolution strategies, we have traversed a landscape rich with challenges and opportunities. From the intricate dynamics of workplace conflicts to the complexities of intimate relationships, societal change, and the digital age, conflict has revealed itself as a multifaceted phenomenon deeply woven into the fabric of human interactions. As we conclude our journey, we pause to reflect on the diversity of conflict resolution challenges we have encountered and the lessons they offer for navigating the complexities of our interconnected world.

Recognizing the Universality of Conflict

One striking realization is the universal nature of conflict. Regardless of setting, culture, or context, conflicts emerge as a natural consequence of diverse perspectives and interests. Acknowledging this universality provides a starting point for effective conflict resolution, as it reminds us that we are not alone in grappling with these challenges.

The Role of Communication and Empathy

Communication and empathy emerge as powerful themes throughout our exploration. Clear communication, both verbal and nonverbal, forms the foundation for addressing conflicts constructively. Empathy, the ability to understand and share the feelings of others, bridges the gap between differing viewpoints and lays the groundwork for mutual understanding.

The Power of Adaptation and Flexibility

Adapting conflict resolution strategies to context is a skill that has proven crucial. What works in one situation may not be effective in another. Flexibility in approach demonstrates the ability to tailor solutions to the unique nuances of each conflict scenario.

Challenges and Opportunities in Technology

Our digital age presents both challenges and opportunities in conflict resolution. While online interactions bring convenience, they also introduce new dimensions of conflict. Learning to navigate conflicts in the digital realm requires a nuanced understanding of online dynamics, digital etiquette, and the potential for misunderstanding.

Conflict as a Catalyst for Change

Conflict, rather than being solely a source of discord, has emerged as a catalyst for positive transformation. We have seen how conflicts can drive change in workplace dynamics, address deeply rooted societal injustices, and inspire collective efforts for a more equitable world.

A Path Forward: Equipped to Navigate Conflict

As we reflect on the diversity of conflict resolution challenges, we recognize that conflict is an inherent part of the human experience. Armed with a toolkit of communication skills, empathy, adaptability, and a commitment to positive transformation, we are better equipped to navigate conflicts in all areas of life. Whether in workplace interactions, family dynamics, intimate relationships, or broader societal contexts, conflict resolution strategies provide a roadmap for navigating disagreements with grace and understanding.

Embracing the Ongoing Journey

Our exploration of conflict resolution is not a destination but a starting point for an ongoing journey. The lessons learned here offer a foundation for continued growth and development as conflict resolvers. As we continue forward, let us remember the importance of fostering dialogue, promoting empathy, advocating for justice, and using the wisdom gained from conflicts to shape a more equitable and harmonious future for ourselves and generations to come.

Equipped to Address Conflict in All Areas of Life

As we draw our exploration of conflict resolution strategies to a close, we find ourselves equipped with a comprehensive toolkit to navigate the myriad challenges that conflicts present in various spheres of life. From the intricacies of workplace dynamics to the complexities of intimate relationships, societal change, and digital interactions, our journey has illuminated the pathways to constructive conflict resolution. In this final section, we reflect on how our newfound insights empower us to address conflict in all areas of life, fostering growth, understanding, and harmony.

The Universality of Conflict Resolution Skills

One of the most striking revelations is the universal applicability of conflict resolution skills. The techniques, principles, and strategies we have uncovered are not confined to specific contexts but can be applied across all facets of life. This universality underscores the importance of acquiring and honing conflict resolution skills as a foundational life skill.

Communication as the Keystone

Communication emerges as the keystone of effective conflict resolution. Whether in the workplace, family, intimate relationships, or broader communities, clear and empathetic communication forms the bedrock upon which conflicts can be addressed constructively. The ability to articulate thoughts, listen actively, and convey understanding transcends boundaries and paves the way for meaningful resolution.

Embracing Diversity and Flexibility

Our journey has emphasized the significance of adapting conflict resolution strategies to diverse contexts. Each situation brings its own nuances, necessitating a flexible approach that considers cultural, emotional, and relational factors. Embracing diversity and fostering an openness to adapt is essential for successful conflict resolution.

Conflict as a Catalyst for Growth

Rather than viewing conflicts as obstacles, we now recognize them as opportunities for growth. Conflicts push us beyond our comfort zones, encouraging us to challenge assumptions, reevaluate perspectives, and embrace discomfort as a catalyst for self-improvement.

Promoting Positive Transformation

At the heart of our exploration lies the potential for conflict to ignite positive transformation. By leveraging conflicts as vehicles for change, we can address longstanding issues, advocate for justice, and contribute to a more equitable and inclusive world.

A Lifelong Journey

Equipped with the wisdom gained from our journey, we embark on a lifelong path of applying conflict resolution strategies. These strategies not only enable us to navigate conflicts but also serve as vehicles for fostering deeper connections, understanding, and empathy with others.

Embracing Conflict as an Opportunity

In closing, our exploration of conflict resolution strategies has imparted a fundamental truth: conflicts are an integral part of the human experience. Rather than shying away from conflicts, we now stand ready to embrace them as opportunities for growth, learning, and positive change. Armed with effective communication, empathy, adaptability, and a commitment to justice, we approach conflicts in all areas of life with a newfound sense of confidence and purpose. As we continue our journey, let us carry forward the lessons learned here, using conflict as a vehicle for personal transformation and a force for creating a more harmonious and just world.

The Ongoing Journey to Becoming a Master Conflict Resolver

As we bring our exploration of conflict resolution strategies to a close, we recognize that this is not the end, but rather the beginning of a lifelong journey toward mastering the art of conflict resolution. The insights we've gained span a vast array of settings, from workplace dynamics to intimate relationships, digital interactions, and societal change. In this concluding section, we reflect on the ongoing journey to becoming a master conflict resolver—a journey that demands dedication, self-awareness, continuous learning, and an unwavering commitment to creating positive change.

A Dynamic Learning Process

Conflict resolution is not a static skill set; it's a dynamic learning process that evolves with our experiences and interactions. Each conflict we encounter provides an opportunity to hone our skills, refine our strategies, and deepen our understanding of human dynamics.

The Role of Self-Awareness

Central to the journey of becoming a master conflict resolver is self-awareness. Understanding our own triggers, biases, and communication styles empowers us to approach conflicts with a sense of clarity and control.

Continuous Learning and Adaptation

Conflict resolution strategies continue to evolve, influenced by psychology, neuroscience, and evolving societal norms. Engaging in continuous learning equips us with the latest tools to address conflicts effectively.

Navigating Complexity and Nuance

Conflict resolution in various settings demands an ability to navigate complexity and nuance. Mastering conflict resolution involves not only understanding interpersonal dynamics but also considering larger systemic factors that contribute to conflicts.

Embracing Constructive Feedback

An essential aspect of growth as a conflict resolver is the willingness to receive and apply constructive feedback. Embracing feedback encourages us to view conflicts as opportunities for improvement rather than failures.

A Commitment to Positive Impact

The journey to becoming a master conflict resolver is not solely for personal growth—it's a commitment to making a positive impact on the world. Each conflict resolved constructively contributes to a more harmonious and just society.

Conclusion: Pioneering a New Way Forward

As we conclude our exploration of conflict resolution strategies, we recognize that the journey to mastery is both challenging and rewarding. By embracing conflicts as learning opportunities, cultivating self-awareness, engaging in continuous learning, navigating complexity, and committing to positive impact, we pioneer a new way forward—one that is guided by empathy, understanding, and a dedication to creating a more harmonious world.

An Invitation to Continuous Growth

In our quest to become master conflict resolvers, we recognize that there will always be new challenges, unforeseen contexts, and uncharted territories. With each conflict we address, we refine our skills, deepen our insights, and contribute to the ongoing evolution of conflict resolution as a field.

Carrying the Torch Forward

As we conclude this chapter, let us remember that conflict resolution is not just a skill; it's a mindset, a philosophy, and a way of engaging with the world. Let us carry the torch forward, inspiring others to navigate conflicts with empathy, to seek understanding before judgment, and to contribute to a world where conflicts are seen as opportunities for growth, transformation, and positive change. Our journey to becoming master conflict resolvers continues, lighting the path for generations to come.

THE END

Wordbook

Welcome to the glossary section of this book. Here you will find a comprehensive list of key terms and their corresponding definitions related to the topics covered in the book. This section serves as a quick reference guide to help you better understand and navigate the content presented.

Key terms

1. Conflict Resolution: The process of addressing and resolving disagreements, disputes, or conflicts between individuals, groups, or entities through communication, negotiation, and cooperation.

2. De-escalation: The practice of reducing the intensity or severity of a conflict or disagreement to prevent it from escalating further and potentially becoming more damaging.

3. Compromise: An approach to conflict resolution where parties involved reach a mutually acceptable agreement by making concessions and finding middle ground.

4. Win-Win Solution: A resolution to a conflict where all parties involved benefit and achieve their objectives, ensuring a positive outcome for everyone.

5. Diversity: The presence of a wide range of differences among individuals, including factors such as culture, background, perspectives, and experiences.

6. Context: The specific circumstances, environment, or situation in which a conflict arises, which can significantly impact the approach to conflict resolution.

7. Adaptation: The process of adjusting conflict resolution strategies to fit the unique characteristics of a particular situation or context.

8. Empathy: The ability to understand and share the feelings and perspectives of others, which plays a crucial role in resolving conflicts constructively.

9. Collaboration: Working together with others to achieve a common goal, often involving a cooperative effort to address conflicts and find solutions.

10. Communication: The exchange of information, ideas, and emotions between individuals or groups, which is essential for effective conflict resolution.

11. Mediation: A process in which a neutral third party facilitates communication and negotiation between conflicting parties to help them reach a resolution.

12. Negotiation: The process of reaching an agreement between conflicting parties through discussions, compromise, and mutual understanding.

13. Resolution Techniques: Various methods and strategies used to address conflicts, including active listening, assertiveness, problem-solving, and reframing.

14. Societal Change: Transformation of broader social structures, norms, and systems that can result from addressing conflicts and advocating for social justice.

15. Empowerment: Providing individuals or groups with the tools, resources, and confidence to address conflicts and make positive changes in their lives and communities.

16. Positive Transformation: The process of turning conflicts into opportunities for growth, learning, and change that lead to improved relationships and environments.

17. Allyship: A commitment to standing in solidarity with marginalized individuals or groups and using one's privilege to support and amplify their voices.

18. Inclusivity: Creating an environment that values and respects the perspectives and contributions of all individuals, fostering a sense of belonging and harmony.

19. Continuous Learning: The ongoing process of acquiring new knowledge, skills, and insights to improve conflict resolution techniques and adapt to evolving situations.

20. Constructive Dialogue: Engaging in open, respectful, and meaningful conversations that promote

understanding, bridge differences, and seek solutions to conflicts.

Supplementary Materials

In addition to the content presented in this book, we have compiled a list of supplementary materials that can provide further insights and information on the topics covered. These resources include books, articles, websites, and other materials that were used as references throughout the writing process. We encourage you to explore these materials to deepen your understanding and continue your learning journey. Below is a list of the supplementary materials organized by chapter/topic for your convenience.

Introduction:

- Hocker, J. L., & Wilmot, W. W. (2018). Interpersonal conflict. Routledge.
- Rahim, M. A. (2002). Toward a theory of managing organizational conflict. The International Journal of Conflict Management, 13(3), 206-235.

Chapter 1: Navigating Workplace Conflicts:

- Thomas, K. W. (1992). Conflict and conflict management: Reflections and update. Journal of organizational behavior, 13(3), 265-274.
- Bolton, R. (2005). People skills: How to assert yourself, listen to others, and resolve conflicts. Simon and Schuster.

Chapter 2: Family Dynamics and Relationships:

- McGoldrick, M., Gerson, R., & Petry, S. (2008). Genograms: Assessment and intervention. WW Norton & Company.
- Gottman, J. M., & Silver, N. (2018). The seven principles for making marriage work. Harmony.

Chapter 3: Intimate Relationships and Partnerships:
- Hendrix, H. (2009). Getting the love you want: A guide for couples. Henry Holt and Company.
- Johnson, S. M. (2008). Hold me tight: Seven conversations for a lifetime of love. Little, Brown Spark.

Chapter 4: Navigating Friendships and Social Circles:
- Fehr, B., & Russell, J. A. (1991). The concept of love viewed from a prototype perspective. Journal of Personality and Social Psychology, 60(3), 425-438.
- Levine, M., & Thompson, L. (2004). Identity, place, and bystander intervention: Social categories and helping after natural disasters. Journal of Social Issues, 60(3), 467-487.

Chapter 5: Promoting Understanding in Communities:
- Deutsch, M., & Coleman, P. T. (Eds.). (2000). The handbook of conflict resolution: Theory and practice. John Wiley & Sons.
- Bercovitch, J., & Jackson, R. (2009). Conflict resolution in the twenty-first century: Principles, methods, and approaches. University of Michigan Press.

Chapter 6: Applying Conflict Resolution to Online Interactions:

- Suler, J. (2004). The online disinhibition effect. Cyberpsychology & behavior, 7(3), 321-326.

- Herring, S. C. (2002). Computer-mediated discourse. Language and the Internet, 61-83.

Chapter 7: Conflict as Catalyst for Societal Change:

- Pruitt, D. G., & Rubin, J. Z. (1986). Social conflict: Escalation, stalemate, and settlement. Random House.

- Galtung, J. (1996). Peace by peaceful means: Peace and conflict, development and civilization. Sage Publications.

Conclusion:

- Ury, W. (2007). The power of positive no: How to say no and still get to yes. Bantam.

- Argyris, C. (1990). Overcoming organizational defenses: Facilitating organizational learning. Prentice Hall.

www.ingramcontent.com/pod-product-compliance
Lightning Source LLC
LaVergne TN
LVHW012112070526
838202LV00056B/5707